# 11 Plus Vocabulary 2000

By

Paul Smith

# Introduction

An extensive vocabulary is one of the most important skills required for 11+ success. Unfortunately, it is also one of the most difficult skills to master, as getting young kids to memorise hundreds of words is easier said than done!

Vocabulary is tested in the 11+ in different ways such as:

- *Synonyms*
- *Antonyms*
- *Spellings*
- *Fill in Blanks*
- *Odd one Out*
- *Missing Letters*

This book contains 100 varied and interesting exercises enabling kids to learn new words and consolidate their learning quickly and efficiently.
Each exercise contains 20 or more different words that have appeared in the 11+ tests in recent past.

Some of the exercises are designed to enable kids to work with **groups of words** with similar/opposite meanings, enabling quicker absorption of whole sets of new words.

**Spellings** are an important, though sometimes ignored, part of 11 plus.
This book has multiple exercises to test vocabulary combined with spellings.

**Answers** to all exercises are provided at the end of the book.

A child should try to do 2 or 3 exercises every day and make note of any new words to be revised later.

## Table of Contents

*1. Antonyms* ...........................................................................................................................*7*

*2. Happy or Sad* .....................................................................................................................*8*

*3. Synonyms* ..........................................................................................................................*9*

*4. Yes and No Game* ...........................................................................................................*10*

*5. Strong or Weak* ..............................................................................................................*11*

*6. Synonyms* ........................................................................................................................*12*

*7. Lots and Few* ..................................................................................................................*13*

*8. Antonyms* .......................................................................................................................*14*

*9. Odd One Out* ..................................................................................................................*15*

*10. Beautiful and Ugly* .......................................................................................................*16*

*11. Synonym* .......................................................................................................................*17*

*12. Synonym* .......................................................................................................................*18*

*13. Forbid or Permit* ..........................................................................................................*19*

*14. Antonym* .......................................................................................................................*20*

*15. Antonyms* .....................................................................................................................*21*

*16. Synonyms* .....................................................................................................................*22*

*17. Smart or Stupid* ...........................................................................................................*23*

*18. Yes or No Game* ...........................................................................................................*24*

*19. Odd One Out* ................................................................................................................*25*

*20. Big or Small* ..................................................................................................................*26*

*21. Antonyms* .....................................................................................................................*27*

*22. Synonyms* .....................................................................................................................*28*

*23. Clean and Dirty* ............................................................................................................*29*

*24. Antonym* .......................................................................................................................*30*

*25. Synonyms* .....................................................................................................................*31*

*26. Similar and Different* ..................................................................................................*32*

*27. Antonyms* .....................................................................................................................*33*

*28. Synonyms* .....................................................................................................................*34*

29. Fresh and Stale ......... 35
30. Odd One Out ......... 36
31. Yes or No Game ......... 37
32. Try and Quit ......... 38
33. Synonyms ......... 39
34. Antonyms ......... 40
35. Problem or Solution ......... 41
36. Odd One Out ......... 42
37. Synonyms ......... 43
38. Luck or Misfortune ......... 44
39. Antonyms ......... 45
40. Synonym ......... 46
41. Loud and Quiet ......... 47
42. Yes or No Game ......... 48
43. Odd One Out ......... 49
44. Synonyms ......... 50
45. Guilty or Innocent ......... 51
46. Antonyms ......... 52
47. Synonym ......... 53
48. Odd One Out ......... 54
49. Antonyms ......... 55
50. Friend or Foe ......... 56
51. Yes or No Game ......... 57
52. Antonyms ......... 58
53. Odd One Out ......... 59
54. Synonym ......... 60
55. Hide and Seek ......... 61
56. Odd One Out ......... 62
57. Yes or No Game ......... 63

58. High and Low ................................................................................. 64
59. Synonym ...................................................................................... 65
60. Antonyms .................................................................................... 66
61. Intense and Shallow .................................................................... 67
62. Yes or No Game .......................................................................... 68
63. Synonym ...................................................................................... 69
64. Odd One Out ............................................................................... 70
65. Synonyms .................................................................................... 71
66. Dark and Light ............................................................................. 72
67. Antonym ...................................................................................... 73
68. Odd One Out ............................................................................... 74
69. Yes or No Game .......................................................................... 75
70. Synonym ...................................................................................... 76
71. Open or Close .............................................................................. 77
72. Odd One Out ............................................................................... 78
73. Yes or No Game .......................................................................... 79
74. Vacant and Occupied ................................................................. 80
75. Synonym ...................................................................................... 81
76. Odd One Out ............................................................................... 82
77. New Year, Old Socks .................................................................. 83
78. Yes or No Game .......................................................................... 84
79. Synonyms .................................................................................... 85
80. Antonym ...................................................................................... 86
81. You May Be Right, But You Could Be Wrong ......................... 87
82. Odd One Out ............................................................................... 88
83. Synonyms .................................................................................... 89
84. Synonyms .................................................................................... 90
85. Yes or No Game .......................................................................... 91
86. Rude and Polite ........................................................................... 92

87. Odd One Out ............................................................................................................ 93
88. Antonym ................................................................................................................ 94
89. Synonym ................................................................................................................ 95
90. Dangerous and Safe ............................................................................................. 96
91. Synonym ................................................................................................................ 97
92. Yes or No Game .................................................................................................... 98
93. You Can Laugh All You Want, or Cry Me a River ............................................ 99
94. Synonym .............................................................................................................. 100
95. Too Far or Very Near .......................................................................................... 101
96. Synonym .............................................................................................................. 102
97. Short and Tall ...................................................................................................... 103
98. Yes or No Game ................................................................................................... 104
99. Synonym .............................................................................................................. 105
100. Remember Me or Forget All About Me ........................................................ 106
Answer Key ................................................................................................................. 107

# 1. Antonyms

**Instruction:** Complete the antonym of the word in bold.

| | | |
|---|---|---|
| 1. | **break** | m _e n_ d |
| 2. | **friend** | f _o e_ |
| 3. | **like** | d _i s l i k_ e |
| 4. | **smile** | f _r o w_ n |
| 5. | **stale** — *Richards* | f _r e s_ h |
| 6. | **safe** | d _a n g e r o u_ s |
| 7. | **begin** | f _i n i s_ h |
| 8. | **past** | f _u t u r_ e |
| 9. | **cry** | l _a u g_ h |
| 10. | **difficult** | e _a s_ y |
| 11. | **better** | w _o r s_ e |
| 12. | **famous** | un _k n o w_ n |
| 13. | **alive** | d _e a_ d |
| 14. | **stay** | le _a v_ e |
| 15. | **stable** | un _s t a b l_ e |
| 16. | **start** | e _n_ d    terminate, arrest, stop |
| 17. | **believe** | do _u b_ t |
| 18. | **pale** | co _l o u r f_ ul |
| 19. | **colossal** | t _i n_ y |
| 20. | **different** | s _a m_ e |

## 2. Happy or Sad

***Instruction:*** Write the matching synonyms from the Word Bank underneath the words in bold.
*(Two words have been done for you)*

### Word Bank

| | | | | |
|---|---|---|---|---|
| cheery | blue | grinning | woeful | beaming |
| woebegone | glum | jolly | gleeful | buoyant |
| merry | forlorn | contented | sunny | upbeat |
| down | depressed | miserable | sorrowful | gloomy |

| **Happy** | **Sad** |
|---|---|
| *cheery* | *blue* |
| merry | ~~grinning~~ |
| jolly | miserable |
| gleeful | down |
| sunny | depressed |
| beaming | sorrowful |
| buoyant | glum |
| upbeat | gloomy |
| contented | forlorn |
| woeful | woebegone |
| grinning | melancholy |

## 3. Synonyms

**Instruction:** Find the word that is closest in meaning to the word in bold. Cross it out.

| | | | | | |
|---|---|---|---|---|---|
| 1. | **absent** | far | true | present | ~~away~~ |
| 2. | **abundant** | ~~copious~~ | scarce | few | declining |
| 3. | **best** | last | evil | worst | ~~greatest~~ |
| 4. | **bent** | ~~warped~~ | straight | right | left |
| 5. | **accept** | forgive | ~~receive~~ | commence | lie |
| 6. | **admit** | conceal | live | ~~disclose~~ | deny |
| 7. | **clear** | opaque | ~~transparent~~ | dark | clean |
| 8. | **calm** | wild | ~~tranquil~~ | care | cook |
| 9. | **kind** | ugly | cruel | ~~friendly~~ | harsh |
| 10. | **cautious** | boring | warm | ~~careful~~ | blend |
| 11. | **forget** | remember | fake | fast | ~~omit~~ |
| 12. | **rectify** | ~~correct~~ | destroy | to build | to command |
| 13. | **paramount** | very important | fake | famous | wide |
| 14. | **tasty** | aesthetic | abundant | ~~delicious~~ | imposing |
| 15. | **enigmatic** | clear | obvious | ~~puzzling~~ | pithy |
| 16. | **cohesion** | shift | climbing | ~~solidarity~~ | independent |
| 17. | **refund** | borrow | take | receive | ~~repay~~ |
| 18. | **domain** | main | ~~area~~ | marketing | internet |
| 19. | **skip** | ~~bypass~~ | notice | insert | introduce |
| 20. | **candid** | anxious | ~~frank~~ | experienced | secretive |

## 4. Yes and No Game

**Instructions:** Write "Yes" in Column B if the words in Column A are antonyms. If they are NOT antonyms, write "No" then write an antonym for the first word. Several antonyms are possible. *(First two questions have been done for you).*

| Column A | Column B |
|---|---|
| 1. lose – find | Yes |
| 2. hard – thick | No. Antonym of hard is soft |
| 3. tall – short | Yes |
| 4. wide – narrow | Yes |
| 5. flat – level | no |
| 6. many – few | yes |
| 7. whine – cry | no |
| 8. round – circular | no |
| 9. poverty – destitution | no |
| 10. ahead – behind | yes |
| 11. little – giant | yes |
| 12. catch – apprehend | no |
| 13. shout – whisper | yes |
| 14. prohibit – protect | no |
| 15. connect – weld | no |
| 16. win – lose | yes |
| 17. unhappy – cheerful | yes |
| 18. dull – fun | no |
| 19. decline – accept | yes |
| 20. rich – opulent | yes |

## 5. Strong or Weak

*Instruction:* Write the matching synonyms from the Word Bank underneath the words in bold.

### Word Bank

| | | | | |
|---|---|---|---|---|
| athletic | powerful | fragile | forceful | sick |
| tough | redoubtable | rickety | stout | delicate |
| brawny | fatigued | flimsy | infirm | solid |
| spent | fit | debilitated | feeble | firm |

| Strong | Weak |
|---|---|
| tough | feeble |
| athletic | spent |
| powerful | redoubtable |
| fit | fatigued |
| brawny | flimsy |
| solid | debilitated |
| firm | infirm |
|  | sick |
| forceful | delicate |
| stout | rickety |
|  | fragile |

# 6. Synonyms

**Instruction:** Complete the synonym of the word in bold.

| | | |
|---|---|---|
| 1. | happen | oc __cu__ r |
| 2. | reject | d __en__ y |
| 3. | coarse | ro __ug__ h |
| 4. | value | wo __rt__ h |
| 5. | old | a __n c i e__ nt |
| 6. | quiet | s __i l e__ nt |
| 7. | rug | ca __r p e__ t |
| 8. | ask | e __n q u i__ re |
| 9. | writer | a __u t h__ or |
| 10. | mix | b __l e n__ d |
| 11. | freedom | l __i b e r__ ty |
| 12. | boredom | mo __n o t o n__ y |
| 13. | place | in __s e__ rt |
| 14. | sweet | su __g a__ ry |
| 15. | small | t __i n__ y |
| 16. | sick | u __n w e__ ll |
| 17. | trick | de __c e i__ ve |
| 18. | brave | co __u r a g e o__ us |
| 19. | truthfulness | h __o n h i s__ ty |
| 20. | maintain | c __o n t i n u__ e |

# 7. Lots and Few

*Instruction:* Write the matching synonyms from the Word Bank underneath the words in bold.

### Word Bank

| plenty | many | lean | meagre | several |
|---|---|---|---|---|
| copious | sparse | rare | scarce | heaps |
| tons | infrequent | little | abundant | paltry |
| slight | myriad | dozens | piles | scant |

| **Lots** | **Few** |
|---|---|
| plenty | little |
| many | lean |
| dozens | |
| several | slight |
| tons | sparse |
| piles | infrequent |
| | scarce |
| ~~rare~~ | paltry |
| heaps | scant |
| abundant | meagre |
| myriad | rare |
| copious | |

## 8. Antonyms

*Instruction:* Find the antonym of the word in bold. Cross it out.

| | | | | | |
|---|---|---|---|---|---|
| 1. | **innocent** | interesting | brave | guilty | plain |
| 2. | **timid** | bald | bold | popular | evil |
| 3. | **simple** | unique | complicated | misleading | brilliant |
| 4. | **thrift** | poverty | extravagance | shop | musical |
| 5. | **blunt** | sharp | plain | blend | swing |
| 6. | **fertile** | gradual | unrefined | sterile | compressed |
| 7. | **noisy** | curious | boring | cold | quiet |
| 8. | **safe** | sane | dull | reliable | hazardous |
| 9. | **polite** | diligent | secure | recent | discourteous |
| 10. | **wrong** | mad | complete | accurate | abundant |
| 11. | **lethargic** | heavy | neat | easy | energetic |
| 12. | **loyal** | unethical | rude | risky | treacherous |
| 13. | **answer** | reply | question | borrow | rejoin |
| 14. | **aspiration** | desire | reward | thought | aimlessness |
| 15. | **push** | play | stop | pull | hit |
| 16. | **ally** | friend | neighbour | soldier | enemy |
| 17. | **always** | sometimes | together | tomorrow | never |
| 18. | **vacant** | certain | occupied | slow | tiresome |
| 19. | **famous** | mindful | popular | obscure | adequate |
| 20. | **regular** | often | subdued | recent | rare |

# 9. Odd One Out

*Instruction:* Find which word is the odd one out. Cross it out.

| | | | | |
|---|---|---|---|---|
| 1. | believe | suppose | reject | trust |
| 2. | attempt | test | adjust | try |
| 3. | forgive | achieve | excuse | pardon |
| 4. | adolescent | mature | grown | adult |
| 5. | stray | cat | kitten | feline |
| 6. | apparel | costume | attire | bare |
| 7. | flood | swamp | outpouring | draught |
| 8. | develop | grow | raise | shrink |
| 9. | well | better | nice | awful |
| 10. | chant | sing | sob | hum |
| 11. | divine | atrocious | ghastly | dreadful |
| 12. | above | underneath | below | beneath |
| 13. | smooth | wrinkle | crinkle | crease |
| 14. | once | forever | always | eternally |
| 15. | silence | scream | tranquil | quiet |
| 16. | obese | overweight | chubby | scrawny |
| 17. | soft | rigid | delicate | tender |
| 18. | lively | active | sickly | alive |
| 19. | famished | ravenous | starved | filled |
| 20. | frequent | seldom | often | repeatedly |

## 10. Beautiful and Ugly

*Instruction:* Write the matching synonyms from the Word Bank underneath the words in bold.

**Word Bank**

| comely | hideous | alluring | exquisite | unsightly |
|---|---|---|---|---|
| attractive | ghastly | pleasant | enthralling | nasty |
| repellent | dazzling | stunning | deformed | gorgeous |
| awful | lovely | grotesque | disgusting | repulsive |

| **Beautiful** | **Ugly** |
|---|---|
| attractive | awful |
| dazzling | hideous |
| lovely | disgusting |
| pleasant | nasty |
| stunning | ghastly |
| comely | repellent |
| gorgeous | ~~alluring~~ |
| ~~repulsive~~ | deformed |
| exquisite | unsightly |
| enthralling | repulsive |
| alluring | |

## 11. Synonym

**Instruction:** Write the matching synonym from the Word Bank on the blank line. *(The first word had been done for you).*

**Word Bank**

| absolve | mediate | valid | traumatic | dilemma |
|---|---|---|---|---|
| elude | contrast | generate | perception | alternative |
| mistake | fluctuate | beneficial | mandatory | infamous |
| scrutiny | sabotage | derive | evaluate | mortify |

*derive — come to an answer*

1. **acquit** — absolve, free someone from guilt
2. **dissimilarity** — contrast
3. **oscillate** — fluctuate — keeps changing - up + down
4. **produce** — generate
5. **conciliate** — mediate
6. **distressing** — traumatic — really upsetting
7. **helpful** — beneficial
8. **sound** — valid — correct
9. **compulsory** — mandatory — have to do it  *(You have 1)*
10. **predicament** — dilemma — can't decide, difficult
11. **insight** — perception
12. **inspection** — scrutiny
13. **evade** — elude — avoid
14. **notorious** — infamous — famous evil person
15. **substitute** — alternative
16. **oversight** — mistake
17. **appraise** — evaluate — assess something - study it
18. **obtain** — derive — find out or get something
19. **humiliate** — mortify — embarrassed/upset
20. **subvert** — sabotage — ruin something

## 12. Synonym

**Instruction:** Find the synonym of the word in bold. Cross it out.

| | | | | | |
|---|---|---|---|---|---|
| 1. | **believe** | tailor | trust | recognize | deny |
| 2. | **greedy** | lovely | voracious | diet | flavoured |
| 3. | **happiness** | contagious | leisure | pleasure | playful |
| 4. | **hardworking** | lazy | mean | diligent | deceitful |
| 5. | **refuse** | accept | acknowledge | reject | return |
| 6. | **major** | minor | trivial | little | significant |
| 7. | **hollow** | solid | star | flow | empty |
| 8. | **sweet** | spirit | honoured | pleasant | mailed |
| 9. | **brag** | boast | show | perform | applause |
| 10. | **give** | take | get | greed | grant |
| 11. | **quick** | far | slow | deep | fast |
| 12. | **tired** | hire | energy | sleepy | extraordinary |
| 13. | **sleepy** | alert | drowsy | bored | aloof |
| 14. | **neat** | expert | deal | tidy | messy |
| 15. | **soft** | muddy | mushy | menace | marshmallow |
| 16. | **mad** | afar | upset | trial | bespoken |
| 17. | **male** | fragile | female | flare | masculine |
| 18. | **malevolent** | fairy | good | better | malicious |
| 19. | **adolescent** | adult | toddler | teenager | adorn |
| 20. | **adult** | spoiled | spare | mature | father |

# 13. Forbid or Permit

*Instruction:* Write the matching synonyms from the Word Bank underneath the words in bold.

### Word Bank

| entitle | enjoin | approve | allow | restrain |
| interdict | ban | grant | outlaw | authorise |
| preclude | prohibit | veto | block | permit |
| let | sanction | disallow | empower | proscribe |

| Forbid | Permit |
|---|---|
| ban | let |
| block | enjoin |
| disallow | allow |
| grant | permit |
| restrain | approve |
| preclude | authorise |
| sanction | entitle |
| proscribe | empower |
| outlaw | prohibit |
| interdict | |
| prohibit | |
| veto | |

## 14. Antonym

**Instruction:** Write the matching antonym from the Word Bank on the blank.

### Word Bank

| implicit | deficient | climb | inclusive | tranquillity |
| begin | inaccurate | converge | deduct | enthusiastic |
| flourish | formidable | agitation | immune | diurnal |
| leave | carnivore | virtuoso | outgoing | protagonist |

1. add — deduct
2. fail — flourish
3. abundant — deficient
4. susceptible — immune
5. apathetic — enthusiastic
6. diverge — converge
7. stay — leave
8. terminate — begin
9. chaos — tranquillity
10. herbivore — carnivore
11. explicit — implicit
12. nocturnal — diurnal
13. exact — inaccurate
14. powerless — formidable
15. exclusive — inclusive
16. antagonist — protagonist
17. descend — climb
18. repose restful — agitation
19. amateur — virtuoso
20. introverted — outgoing

## 15. Antonyms

*Instruction:* Complete the antonym of the word in bold.

1. **boastful** — mo_d__e__s_t
2. **fragile** — re _ _ _ _ _ _ nt
3. **clumsy** — gr_a__s__e__f_ul
4. **attract** — r_e__p_el
5. **clean-shaven** — b_e__a__r__d_ed
6. **approach** — le_a__v_e
7. **introverted** — o_u__t__g__o__i__n_g
8. **offer** — ac_c__e__p_t
9. **ornate** — p_l__a__i_n
10. **poverty** — l_u__x__u__r_y
11. **get** — g_i__v_e
12. **absent** — p_r__e__s__e_nt
13. **defence** — of_f__e__n__s_e
14. **improve** — de _ _ _ _ _ _ _ te
15. **stick by** — ab_a__n__d_on
16. **broad** — na_r__r__o_w
17. **risky** — s_a__f_e
18. **appear** — v_a__n__i_sh
19. **allow** — pr_e__v__e__n_t
20. **useful** — u_s__e__l__e_ss

## 16. Synonyms

**Instruction:** Find the synonym of the word in bold. Cross it out.

| | | | | | |
|---|---|---|---|---|---|
| 1. | **humble** | modest | illiterate | trying | prone |
| 2. | **loud** | siren | deafening | proud | quiet |
| 3. | **modern** | old-fashioned | contemporary | interesting | daily |
| 4. | **rich** | healthy | wealthy | poor | hearty |
| 5. | **sceptic** | trusting | trustful | try | cynic |
| 6. | **lie** | encourage | truth | stand | untruth |
| 7. | **pail** | dim | dark | bucket | straight |
| 8. | **stay** | go | leave | wait | learn |
| 9. | **down** | upright | cheery | unhappy | delay |
| 10. | **cover** | expose | choose | protect | explain |
| 11. | **intelligent** | quick-witted | dull | dumb | shrink |
| 12. | **tough** | strong | weak | denial | abandon |
| 13. | **alert** | expensive | inattentive | vigilant | stray |
| 14. | **disclosure** | state | revelation | blunt | sentence |
| 15. | **fight** | build | brawl | take | left |
| 16. | **arrange** | ahead | organise | district | attend |
| 17. | **distract** | allow | deny | divert | invert |
| 18. | **control** | command | plus | convey | convert |
| 19. | **hold** | grow | grasp | ground | grit |
| 20. | **agree** | actress | accept | account | accommodate |

## 17. Smart or Stupid

*Instruction:* Write the matching synonyms from the Word Bank underneath the words in bold.

### Word Bank

| clever | ignorant | foolish | savvy | ludicrous |
|---|---|---|---|---|
| thick | perceptive | brainy | dumb | alert |
| sharp | bright | mindless | intelligent | genius |
| brainless | imbecile | brilliant | silly | dummy |

| **Smart** | **Stupid** |
|---|---|
| clever | brainless |
| perceptive | ignorant |
| sharp | imbecile |
| bright | foolish |
| brilliant | mindless |
| intelligent | dumb |
| genious | silly |
| brainy | dummy |
| alert | ludicrous |
| savvy | thick |

## 18. Yes or No Game

***Instructions:*** Write "Yes" in Column B if the words in Column A are synonyms. If they are NOT synonyms, write "No" then write a synonym for the first word. Several synonyms are possible.

| Column A | Column B |
|---|---|
| 1. accelerate – quicken | yes |
| 2. oblivious – aware | no |
| 3. hasten – dawdle | no |
| 4. pliable – rigid | no |
| 5. blatant – subtle | no |
| 6. tentative – definite | no |
| 7. hot – lukewarm | no |
| 8. metropolis – city | yes |
| 9. up – alert | no |
| 10. cold – chilly | yes |
| 11. baby – infant | yes |
| 12. serene – town | no |
| 13. silent – quiet | yes |
| 14. affection – fondness | yes |
| 15. odour – mild | no |
| 16. master – slave | no |
| 17. liberty – freedom | yes |
| 18. alliance – league | yesg |
| 19. decision – conflict | no |
| 20. guilty - innocent | no |

# 19. Odd One Out

**Instruction:** Find which word is the odd one out. Cross it out.

| | | | | |
|---|---|---|---|---|
| 1. | affection | hate | love | like |
| 2. | help | aid | belittle | assist |
| 3. | forget | forgive | ignore | neglect |
| 4. | enemy | challenger | antagonist | brother |
| 5. | stay | allow | remain | wait |
| 6. | virtue | decency | righteousness | immorality |
| 7. | pull | push | pluck | yank |
| 8. | decrease | descent | decline | desire |
| 9. | absent | present | lacking | gone |
| 10. | team | group | class | classroom |
| 11. | joke | trick | prank | error |
| 12. | stress | tension | prediction | pressure |
| 13. | idea | liability | thought | concept |
| 14. | one | two | letter | three |
| 15. | golden | gilded | riches | ancient |
| 16. | overtired | fatigued | weary | enthusiastic |
| 17. | credence | scepticism | faith | trust |
| 18. | promptness | tardiness | late | delay |
| 19. | tools | equipment | attic | gear |
| 20. | repetition | replication | recurrence | remorse |

## 20. Big or Small

***Instruction:*** Write the matching synonyms from the Word Bank underneath the words in bold.

**Word Bank**

| substantial | petite | tiny | great | enormous |
| huge | slight | mighty | gigantic | colossal |
| diminutive | compact | insignificant | stupendous | massive |
| minuscule | microscopic | jumbo | baby | miniature |

**Big** | **Small**

# 21. Antonyms

***Instruction:*** Complete the antonym of the word in bold.

1. **important**     i r ___ ___ ___ ___ ___ ___ n t
2. **full**     e ___ ___ ___ y
3. **disappointed**     s a ___ ___ ___ ___ ___ e d
4. **forever**     t ___ ___ ___ ___ ___ ___ r y
5. **abundant**     s p ___ ___ ___ e
6. **fake**     o r ___ ___ ___ ___ ___ l
7. **serious**     t r ___ ___ ___ ___ l
8. **false**     t ___ ___ e
9. **supply**     d e ___ ___ ___ d
10. **black**     w ___ ___ ___ e
11. **reduce**     i n ___ ___ ___ ___ ___ e
12. **occupied**     v a ___ ___ ___ t
13. **cruel**     m e ___ ___ ___ ___ ___ l
14. **leave**     s ___ ___ y
15. **for**     a g ___ ___ ___ ___ t
16. **pro**     c ___ n
17. **abstract**     c o ___ ___ ___ ___ t e
18. **general**     s p ___ ___ ___ ___ ___ c
19. **day**     n ___ ___ ___ t
20. **freeze**     m ___ ___ t

## 22. Synonyms

***Instruction:*** Find the synonym of the word in bold. Cross it out.

| | | | | | |
|---|---|---|---|---|---|
| 1. | **add** | remove | include | deduct | reduce |
| 2. | **buy** | sell | sale | purchase | review |
| 3. | **fear** | tired | fire | fright | belief |
| 4. | **sit** | perch | stand | rise | device |
| 5. | **late** | on time | delayed | beneath | below |
| 6. | **inside** | outer | outside | inner | public |
| 7. | **admit** | reflect | remember | try | confess |
| 8. | **more** | less | fewer | additional | old |
| 9. | **bring** | follow | quit | carry | leave |
| 10. | **catch** | seize | dozen | correlate | respond |
| 11. | **horror** | idea | terror | magnitude | drop |
| 12. | **arrive** | come | leave | call | step |
| 13. | **real** | ideal | imaginary | fake | actual |
| 14. | **motion** | stand | sit | movement | word |
| 15. | **avoid** | indulge | confront | ignore | oppose |
| 16. | **love** | hate | heal | treat | adore |
| 17. | **fail** | work | walk | flunk | sail |
| 18. | **ready** | give | prepared | testing | trait |
| 19. | **best** | pot | greatest | belittle | friend |
| 20. | **similar** | alike | aloof | apart | different |

# 23. Clean and Dirty

***Instruction:*** Write the matching synonyms from the Word Bank underneath the words in bold.

**Word Bank**

| unsoiled | filthy | washed | mucky | nasty |
|---|---|---|---|---|
| tidy | pure | spotless | scrubbed | greasy |
| unstained | contaminated | icky | sanitary | hygienic |
| stained | cleansed | foul | obscene | grimy |

| **Clean** | **Dirty** |
|---|---|
|  |  |
|  |  |
|  |  |
|  |  |
|  |  |
|  |  |
|  |  |
|  |  |
|  |  |
|  |  |

## 24. Antonym

***Instruction:*** Write the matching antonym from the Word Bank on the blank.

**Word Bank**

| theory | asset | absence | belief | departure |
| take off | uphill | liquid | exit | safety |
| allegiance | proof | proximity | land | different |
| deport | import | anonymous | primary | inferior |

1. **downhill** _____
2. **landing** _____
3. **fact** _____
4. **liability** _____
5. **admit** _____
6. **treason** _____
7. **entrance** _____
8. **sea** _____
9. **identical** _____
10. **presence** _____
11. **export** _____
12. **solid** _____
13. **danger** _____
14. **secondary** _____
15. **disbelief** _____
16. **superior** _____
17. **famous** _____
18. **arrival** _____
19. **guess** _____
20. **distance** _____

## 25. Synonyms

**Instruction:** Complete the synonym of the word in bold.

| 1. | share | s p _ _ t |
| 2. | simple | p _ _ i n |
| 3. | win | t r _ _ _ _ h |
| 4. | vacation | h o _ _ _ _ y |
| 5. | property | b e _ _ _ _ _ _ g s |
| 6. | anguish | d i _ _ _ _ s s |
| 7. | stop | c e _ _ e |
| 8. | cruelty | b r _ _ _ _ _ t y |
| 9. | old | e l _ _ _ _ y |
| 10. | vote | b a _ _ _ t |
| 11. | receive | o b _ _ _ n |
| 12. | nation | c _ _ _ _ r y |
| 13. | study | l e _ _ n |
| 14. | contemporary | c _ _ _ _ n t |
| 15. | mission | q u _ _ t |
| 16. | young | y o _ _ _ _ u l |
| 17. | malicious | m a _ _ _ _ _ _ n t |
| 18. | tell | i _ _ _ _ m |
| 19. | film | m _ _ _ e |
| 20. | wrong | i n _ _ _ _ _ _ t |

# 26. Similar and Different

***Instruction:*** Write the matching synonyms from the Word Bank underneath the words in bold.

**Word Bank**

| discrete | disparate | individual | comparable | equivalent |
|---|---|---|---|---|
| matching | dissimilar | akin | alike | incompatible |
| close | related | homogeneous | unusual | contrasting |
| analogous | resembling | distinct | inconsistent | diverse |

| **Similar** | **Different** |
|---|---|
| | |
| | |
| | |
| | |
| | |
| | |
| | |
| | |
| | |
| | |
| | |
| | |

# 27. Antonyms

**Instruction:** Complete the antonym of the word in bold.

| | | |
|---|---|---|
| 1. | **wrong** | c o _ _ _ _ t |
| 2. | **dry** | h _ _ _ d |
| 3. | **here** | t h _ _ e |
| 4. | **liquid** | s o _ _ d |
| 5. | **minimum** | m a _ _ _ _ m |
| 6. | **everybody** | n _ _ _ _ y |
| 7. | **tomorrow** | y e _ _ _ _ _ _ y |
| 8. | **present** | a b _ _ _ t |
| 9. | **suburb** | c _ _ _ r e |
| 10. | **exactly** | a p _ _ _ _ _ _ _ _ _ y |
| 11. | **dead** | a _ _ _ e |
| 12. | **exemplary** | o u _ _ _ _ _ _ u s |
| 13. | **unite** | d i _ _ _ e |
| 14. | **hell** | h _ _ _ _ n |
| 15. | **top** | b _ _ _ _ m |
| 16. | **master** | s _ _ _ _ n t |
| 17. | **private** | p _ _ _ _ c |
| 18. | **foreigner** | n a _ _ _ e |
| 19. | **best** | w _ _ _ t |
| 20. | **teach** | l e _ _ n |

## 28. Synonyms

**Instruction:** Find the synonym of the word in bold. Cross it out.

| | | | | | |
|---|---|---|---|---|---|
| 1. | **illness** | toothache | sickness | sailor | ship |
| 2. | **monotony** | party | adventure | dullness | drowsy |
| 3. | **peril** | jeopardy | safety | maps | diver |
| 4. | **occasionally** | now | tomorrow | sometimes | later |
| 5. | **reek** | perfume | aroma | stink | permit |
| 6. | **tedious** | fun | boring | exciting | biting |
| 7. | **vulnerable** | homeless | endangered | above | resilient |
| 8. | **anguish** | pleasantry | surprise | suffice | suffering |
| 9. | **wary** | attention | trustful | inattentive | cautious |
| 10. | **keen** | allow | mean | keep | eager |
| 11. | **woods** | trees | forest | mountain | field |
| 12. | **revengeful** | lazy | salute | vindictive | tedious |
| 13. | **panorama** | interior | scene | congestion | camera |
| 14. | **supervise** | alarm | direct | follow | neglect |
| 15. | **devotion** | convenient | deduct | reduce | loyalty |
| 16. | **happiness** | flaw | boredom | joy | wonder |
| 17. | **sleeplessness** | dreaming | insomnia | nightmare | apnea |
| 18. | **show** | deteriorate | demonstrate | attend | devotion |
| 19. | **eliminate** | colic | eradicate | convince | extreme |
| 20. | **violently** | strict | forcefully | peacefully | rigorous |

## 29. Fresh and Stale

***Instruction:*** Write the matching synonyms from the Word Bank underneath the words in bold.

### Word Bank

| uncured | old | new | rotten | natural |
| spoiled | unspoiled | pristine | original | off |
| hardened | pure | unprocessed | rancid | unpreserved |
| decayed | dry | clean | musty | timeworn |

| **Fresh** | **Stale** |
|---|---|
| | |
| | |
| | |
| | |
| | |
| | |
| | |
| | |
| | |
| | |

# 30. Odd One Out

**Instruction:** Find which word is the odd one out. Cross it out.

| | | | | |
|---|---|---|---|---|
| 1. | closest | near | here | outside |
| 2. | dirty | filthy | clean | stained |
| 3. | message | data | information | book |
| 4. | wish | desire | will | wound |
| 5. | heal | injure | hurt | pain |
| 6. | shine | sparkle | clean | musty |
| 7. | destroy | demolish | derive | damage |
| 8. | similar | equal | alike | apart |
| 9. | relative | cousin | family | neighbour |
| 10. | commence | finish | start | begin |
| 11. | loyal | true | treacherous | faithful |
| 12. | colourful | monochrome | animated | vivid |
| 13. | spectrum | rainbow | iridescent | unicorn |
| 14. | express | speedy | superb | fast |
| 15. | dusk | sunrise | evening | night |
| 16. | inside | inaugurate | inner | indoors |
| 17. | prudent | youthful | young | juvenile |
| 18. | proud | limit | restrict | ban |
| 19. | watch | observe | see | outburst |
| 20. | wreck | repair | mend | restore |

## 31. Yes or No Game

**Instructions:** Write "Yes" in Column B if the words in Column A are synonyms. If they are NOT synonyms, write "No" then write a synonym for the first word. Several synonyms are possible.

| Column A | Column B |
|---|---|
| 1. scare – frighten | |
| 2. bald – bold | |
| 3. silly – foolish | |
| 4. stinky – aroma | |
| 5. run – stop | |
| 6. nice – delightful | |
| 7. rare – uncommon | |
| 8. inside – within | |
| 9. without – whether | |
| 10. rapid – fast | |
| 11. pal – foe | |
| 12. near – distant | |
| 13. wise – wide | |
| 14. wild – tame | |
| 15. insipid – interesting | |
| 16. automatic – car | |
| 17. elephantine – mammoth | |
| 18. illusionist – magician | |
| 19. applaud - clap | |
| 20. audience - spectators | |

## 32. Try and Quit

***Instruction:*** Write the matching synonyms from the Word Bank underneath the words in bold.

**Word Bank**

| test | retire | withdraw | attempt | leave |
| seek | abandon | strive | aspire | cease |
| drop | effort | taste | endeavour | check |
| left | experiment | desert | discontinue | resign |

| **Try** | **Quit** |
| --- | --- |
| | |

## 33. Synonyms

**Instruction:** Complete the synonym of the word in bold.

| | | |
|---|---|---|
| 1. | **kind** | n ___ ___ e |
| 2. | **complex** | c o ___ ___ ___ ___ ___ ___ ___ e d |
| 3. | **glad** | p l ___ ___ ___ e d |
| 4. | **noisy** | l ___ ___ d |
| 5. | **tiny** | p e ___ ___ t e |
| 6. | **lady** | w ___ ___ ___ n |
| 7. | **sad** | u n ___ ___ ___ ___ y |
| 8. | **huge** | e n ___ ___ ___ ___ s |
| 9. | **interesting** | f a ___ ___ ___ ___ ___ ___ n g |
| 10. | **strange** | u n ___ ___ ___ ___ l |
| 11. | **loose** | b a ___ ___ y |
| 12. | **very hot** | s c ___ ___ ___ ___ ___ ___ g |
| 13. | **squander** | w ___ ___ t e |
| 14. | **ridiculous** | a b ___ ___ ___ d |
| 15. | **gigantic** | h ___ ___ e |
| 16. | **cautious** | c a ___ ___ ___ ___ l |
| 17. | **differ** | d i ___ ___ ___ ___ e e |
| 18. | **fearless** | b ___ ___ v e |
| 19. | **achieve** | s u ___ ___ ___ ___ d |
| 20. | **irritate** | a n ___ ___ y |

## 34. Antonyms

**Instruction:** Find the antonym of the word in bold. Cross it out.

| | | | | | |
|---|---|---|---|---|---|
| 1. | **live** | lie | die | deny | cry |
| 2. | **complete** | entire | partial | fraud | depart |
| 3. | **summer** | day | spring | winter | autumn |
| 4. | **dirty** | heavy | clan | true | clean |
| 5. | **first** | second | last | minute | later |
| 6. | **sob** | cry | laugh | accept | cold |
| 7. | **destroy** | cover | peace | build | war |
| 8. | **sick** | hard | ill | healthy | poor |
| 9. | **rare** | common | contrast | command | convoy |
| 10. | **reliable** | isolate | trusting | friend | untrustworthy |
| 11. | **mend** | qualify | destroy | centre | bend |
| 12. | **firm** | bleed | bond | tough | soft |
| 13. | **odd** | unusual | peculiar | normal | strange |
| 14. | **injustice** | fairness | fight | wrong | freedom |
| 15. | **war** | cry | fight | soldier | peace |
| 16. | **fat** | obese | skinny | grand | great |
| 17. | **man** | boy | masculine | woman | guy |
| 18. | **old** | pension | retired | youthful | scar |
| 19. | **far** | close | there | behind | below |
| 20. | **city** | country | town | centre | market |

# 35. Problem or Solution

*Instruction:* Write the matching synonyms from the Word Bank underneath the words in bold.

**Word Bank**

| trouble | result | issue | answer | challenge |
|---|---|---|---|---|
| determination | difficulty | finding | solving | key |
| complication | explication | worry | nuisance | obstacle |
| predicament | conclusion | concern | resolution | explanation |

| **Problem** | **Solution** |
|---|---|
| | |
| | |
| | |
| | |
| | |
| | |
| | |
| | |
| | |
| | |

# 36. Odd One Out

**Instruction:** Find which word is the odd one out. Cross it out.

| | | | | |
|---|---|---|---|---|
| 1. | dear | kind | nice | nasty |
| 2. | mindful | brilliant | thankful | smart |
| 3. | irritate | agitate | accurate | annoy |
| 4. | sell | buy | purchase | acquire |
| 5. | deal | break | contract | agreement |
| 6. | among | apart | separately | independently |
| 7. | steel | pierce | slit | cut |
| 8. | pair | couple | match | dice |
| 9. | live | recede | dwell | reside |
| 10. | remote | aloof | distant | friendly |
| 11. | fiction | information | data | facts |
| 12. | end | abort | commence | terminate |
| 13. | error | missile | mistake | misconception |
| 14. | launch | introduce | instigate | shift |
| 15. | mellow | amicable | deluxe | warm |
| 16. | era | condition | period | epoch |
| 17. | situation | style | circumstances | state |
| 18. | mushroom | bacteria | germs | bacilli |
| 19. | heal | rehabilitate | heat | remedy |
| 20. | blow | whistle | toot | shiver |

## 37. Synonyms

**Instruction:** Complete the synonym of the word in bold.

| | | |
|---|---|---|
| 1. | remote | d _ _ _ _ n t |
| 2. | kin | r e _ _ _ _ _ e |
| 3. | gracious | p l _ _ _ _ _ t |
| 4. | impersonator | i _ _ _ _ _ e r |
| 5. | drag | p _ _ l |
| 6. | wary | c _ _ _ _ _ u s |
| 7. | loot | s p _ _ l s |
| 8. | propose | s u _ _ _ s t |
| 9. | prolong | e x _ _ _ d |
| 10. | modest | h _ _ _ e |
| 11. | fearless | b _ _ _ e |
| 12. | beneficial | h e _ _ _ u l |
| 13. | resolve | s e _ _ l e |
| 14. | dupe | d e _ _ _ _ e |
| 15. | reside | d _ _ _ l |
| 16. | gathering | m e _ _ _ n g |
| 17. | bespoke | t a _ _ _ _ e d |
| 18. | aloof | d i _ _ _ _ t |
| 19 | negligent | c a _ _ _ _ _ s |
| 20. | fire | b l _ _ e |

## 38. Luck or Misfortune

**Instruction:** Write the matching synonyms from the Word Bank underneath the words in bold.

### Word Bank

| fortune | calamity | chance | mishap | fate |
| destiny | misery | catastrophe | serendipity | fluke |
| tribulation | disaster | fortuity | difficulty | providence |
| windfall | hardship | tragedy | setback | happenstance |

| **Luck** | **Misfortune** |
|---|---|
|  |  |
|  |  |
|  |  |
|  |  |
|  |  |
|  |  |
|  |  |
|  |  |
|  |  |
|  |  |

## 39. Antonyms

**Instruction:** Find the antonym of the word in bold. Cross it out.

| | | | | | |
|---|---|---|---|---|---|
| 1. | **maintain** | murder | stab | kill | neglect |
| 2. | **ascend** | leap | grow | mount | sink |
| 3. | **revulsion** | delight | violence | disgust | avenge |
| 4. | **servant** | master | slavish | labourer | attendant |
| 5. | **distinctive** | common | divide | deny | different |
| 6. | **angry** | troubled | irritable | difficult | calm |
| 7. | **grit** | bold | cowardice | grease | level |
| 8. | **callous** | hot-tempered | immature | hollow | compassionate |
| 9. | **astute** | quick-witted | clever | charming | stupid |
| 10. | **combat** | fight | conflict | quarrel | peace |
| 11. | **innocent** | steal | guilty | fault | major |
| 12. | **subtle** | carefree | artistic | obvious | nice |
| 13. | **modest** | humble | straight | boastful | shy |
| 14. | **dull** | trying | interesting | malevolent | boredom |
| 15. | **shrink** | tall | playful | expand | extent |
| 16. | **bitter** | coarse | quiet | sweet | enigma |
| 17. | **glow** | fire | flare | darkness | light |
| 18. | **reward** | praise | award | punish | plain |
| 19. | **final** | initial | mandatory | clever | exit |
| 20. | **agree** | rebound | recover | reduce | reject |

## 40. Synonym

**Instruction:** Write the matching synonym from the Word Bank on the blank.

**Word Bank**

| kind | follow | emit | hide | gather |
|---|---|---|---|---|
| fake | mercy | result | fair | dissipate |
| agitate | adversity | weak | attentive | brute |
| shortage | talk | display | brief | impure |

1. frail _____
2. disguise _____
3. accumulate _____
4. calamity _____
5. savage _____
6. alert _____
7. disperse _____
8. humane _____
9. disturb _____
10. pursue _____
11. consequence _____
12. spurious _____
13. deficiency _____
14. speak _____
15. discharge _____
16. polluted _____
17. short _____
18. compassion _____
19. exhibit _____
20. equitable _____

# 41. Loud and Quiet

***Instruction:*** Write the matching synonyms from the Word Bank underneath the words in bold.

**Word Bank**

| peace | noisy | deafening | boisterous | tranquil |
| roaring | rowdy | placid | blaring | clamorous |
| subdued | silent | thunderous | pacify | resounding |
| still | hush | serene | soundless | ear-splitting |

| **Loud** | **Quiet** |
|---|---|
| | |
| | |
| | |
| | |
| | |
| | |
| | |
| | |
| | |
| | |

## 42. Yes or No Game

**Instructions:** Write "Yes" in Column B if the words in Column A are antonyms. If they are NOT antonyms, write "No" then write an antonym for the first word. Several antonyms are possible.

| Column A | Column B |
|---|---|
| 1. strive – attempt | |
| 2. peculiar – ordinary | |
| 3. large – miniature | |
| 4. remain – go | |
| 5. hurriedly – quietly | |
| 6. allow – prevent | |
| 7. cover – expose | |
| 8. humane – home | |
| 9. comfort – distress | |
| 10. curious – cured | |
| 11. assemble – scatter | |
| 12. delighted – cheerful | |
| 13. enmity – hatred | |
| 14. blossom – decay | |
| 15. guest – host | |
| 16. reveal – conceal | |
| 17. ascend – fall | |
| 18. boastful – modest | |
| 19. discontinue – deny | |
| 20. forceful – wimpy | |

## 43. Odd One Out

**Instruction:** Find which word is the odd one out. Cross it out.

| | | | | |
|---|---|---|---|---|
| 1. | useless | vain | futile | conflict |
| 2. | invader | guest | assailant | attacker |
| 3. | lower | inferior | upper | subordinate |
| 4. | friendship | apathy | indifference | unconcern |
| 5. | bold | brave | darling | daring |
| 6. | doubt | distrust | disbelief | disregard |
| 7. | uneven | rough | irregular | smooth |
| 8. | misunderstand | misinterpret | misapprehend | misuse |
| 9. | receive | collect | hoard | gather |
| 10. | firm | hard | ribbon | rigid |
| 11. | joy | delight | plea | pleasure |
| 12. | confine | detain | announce | imprison |
| 13. | unity | division | disunity | conflict |
| 14. | harmful | great | defective | spoiled |
| 15. | awake | asleep | drowsy | dreaming |
| 16. | road | street | boulevard | traffic |
| 17. | prosperity | riches | poverty | success |
| 18. | victory | win | accomplish | defeat |
| 19. | petite | gross | slim | tiny |
| 20. | gradual | hurried | quick | prompt |

## 44. Synonyms

***Instruction:*** Complete the synonym of the word in bold.

| | | | |
|---|---|---|---|
| 1. | **riches** | w ___ ___ ___ t h | |
| 2. | **power** | f o ___ ___ e | |
| 3. | **music** | m e ___ ___ ___ y | |
| 4. | **look** | w ___ ___ c h | |
| 5. | **assist** | h ___ ___ p | |
| 6. | **hop** | j ___ ___ p | |
| 7. | **award** | p r ___ ___ e | |
| 8. | **brilliant** | d a ___ ___ ___ ___ n g | |
| 9. | **cautious** | c a ___ ___ ___ ___ l | |
| 10. | **celebration** | p ___ ___ ___ y | |
| 11. | **affect** | t o ___ ___ h | |
| 12. | **end** | f ___ ___ ___ s h | |
| 13. | **money** | c ___ ___ h | |
| 14. | **glossy** | s h ___ ___ y | |
| 15. | **sad** | g l ___ ___ m y | |
| 16. | **confined** | c r ___ ___ ___ e d | |
| 17. | **crisp** | c r ___ ___ ___ ___ y | |
| 18. | **amazement** | w ___ ___ ___ e r | |
| 19. | **wash** | b ___ ___ h e | |
| 20. | **victory** | s ___ ___ ___ ___ s s | |

# 45. Guilty or Innocent

***Instruction:*** Write the matching synonyms from the Word Bank underneath the words in bold.

**Word Bank**

| ashamed | responsible | untainted | pure | culpable |
| naive | contrite | remorseful | blameless | sinful |
| blameable | repentant | chaste | inoffensive | convicted |
| vindicated | acquitted | criminal | faultless | exonerated |

| **Guilty** | **Innocent** |
| --- | --- |
| | |
| | |
| | |
| | |
| | |
| | |
| | |
| | |
| | |
| | |

## 46. Antonyms

**Instruction:** Find the antonym of the word in bold. Cross it out.

| | | | | | |
|---|---|---|---|---|---|
| 1. | **father** | daddy | papa | mother | priest |
| 2. | **intuition** | clairvoyance | instinct | divination | intellect |
| 3. | **miss** | skip | forget | hit | pay |
| 4. | **sister** | nurse | nun | chum | brother |
| 5. | **modern** | modest | older | contemporary | early |
| 6. | **several** | few | away | timid | many |
| 7. | **ask** | answer | data | correct | information |
| 8. | **long** | large | giant | short | shallow |
| 9. | **husband** | adult | woman | man | wife |
| 10. | **desperate** | serious | depressed | hopeful | hopeless |
| 11. | **order** | law | force | chaos | line |
| 12. | **awake** | wide | dire | asleep | ahead |
| 13. | **heat** | hot | summer | winter | cold |
| 14. | **keep** | give up | retain | hold on to | remain |
| 15. | **constant** | equal | changeable | alike | stall |
| 16. | **later** | delay | deny | earlier | faster |
| 17. | **angel** | devil | pretty | church | sin |
| 18. | **children** | kids | adults | infants | babies |
| 19. | **affirmative** | close | negative | forward | hopeful |
| 20. | **all** | few | none | million | less |

# 47. Synonym

***Instruction:*** Write the matching synonym from the Word Bank on the blank.

**Word Bank**

| view | marvel | terrible | emergency | manage |
| hit | return | evening | cook | nothing |
| sweet | stimulating | destroy | belittle | known |
| wet | genuine | kind | exaggerate | train |

1. crisis _____
2. popular _____
3. sight _____
4. real _____
5. hospitable _____
6. exciting _____
7. sugary _____
8. discipline _____
9. control _____
10. ghastly _____
11. bake _____
12. overstate _____
13. miracle _____
14. demolish _____
15. smack _____
16. moist _____
17. revisit _____
18. disparage _____
19. dusk _____
20. nil _____

# 48. Odd One Out

**Instruction:** Find which word is the odd one out. Cross it out.

| | | | | |
|---|---|---|---|---|
| 1. | foreign | alien | stranger | host |
| 2. | evaluate | detailed | appraise | consider |
| 3. | territory | district | finite | region |
| 4. | reflection | mistake | failure | error |
| 5. | punctual | right | incomparable | exact |
| 6. | complex | intricate | wicked | complicated |
| 7. | compound | indicate | show | imply |
| 8. | fright | battle | combat | fight |
| 9. | fracture | break | crack | squeak |
| 10. | create | diminutive | produce | generate |
| 11. | area | zone | lot | neutral |
| 12. | honour | respect | default | appreciate |
| 13. | rigid | soft | gentle | smooth |
| 14. | stretch | shorten | compress | compact |
| 15. | isolated | determined | faraway | distant |
| 16. | mundane | likely | possible | probable |
| 17. | hail | applaud | appraise | advertise |
| 18. | fake | fragile | fraud | phony |
| 19. | unnatural | abnormal | irregular | irrelevant |
| 20. | impediment | spread | broadcast | distribute |

## 49. Antonyms

**Instruction:** Find the antonym of the word in bold. Cross it out.

| | | | | |
|---|---|---|---|---|
| 1. **hard** | melting | soft | dry | powder |
| 2. **lose** | invent | find | misplace | deny |
| 3. **under** | behind | above | below | last |
| 4. **cold** | delicious | freezing | warm | wet |
| 5. **short** | sharp | small | tall | little |
| 6. **messy** | curious | organised | tired | bored |
| 7. **dark** | down | sun | light | deep |
| 8. **late** | early | behind | tight | correct |
| 9. **empty** | soft | hard | full | dry |
| 10. **close** | try | near | adjacent | far |
| 11. **wet** | silly | moist | spray | dry |
| 12. **small** | entire | enormous | adequate | portable |
| 13. **near** | nearby | at hand | far | approach |
| 14. **heavy** | rude | hefty | thick | light |
| 15. **wide** | spacious | large | vast | narrow |
| 16. **far** | near | distant | remote | away |
| 17. **fast** | lively | slow | swift | rapidly |
| 18. **hungry** | full | starving | hollow | thirsty |
| 19. **intelligent** | clever | brilliant | dumb | sharp |
| 20. **exit** | entrance | end | withdrawal | depart |

# 50. Friend or Foe

**Instruction:** Write the matching synonyms from the Word Bank underneath the words in bold.

| Word Bank | | | | |
|---|---|---|---|---|
| enemy | opponent | buddy | companion | rival |
| ally | comrade | mate | attacker | pal |
| associate | competitor | fellow | partner | antagonist |
| supporter | adversary | challenger | arch-enemy | disputant |

| **Friend** | **Foe** |
|---|---|
| | |

# 51. Yes or No Game

**Instructions:** Write "Yes" beside the word in bold if they are antonyms. If they are NOT antonyms, write "No" then write an antonym for the first word. Several antonyms are possible.

| Column 1 | Column 2 |
|---|---|
| 1. attentive – ahead | |
| 2. slim – fat | |
| 3. thin – narrow | |
| 4. sick – healthy | |
| 5. banish – invite | |
| 6. bluff – truth | |
| 7. attack – strike | |
| 8. diminish – extend | |
| 9. emerge – disappear | |
| 10. furtive – secret | |
| 11. luminous – shiny | |
| 12. multitude – hundreds | |
| 13. persistent – stubborn | |
| 14. pristine – pure | |
| 15. replenish – empty | |
| 16. scarce – lots | |
| 17. scurry – amble | |
| 18. sociable – introverted | |
| 19. unsightly – pleasant | |
| 20. vigilant – disinterested | |

## 52. Antonyms

**Instruction:** Complete the antonym of the word in bold.

|  |  |  |
|---|---|---|
| 1. | **affirm** | d ___ ___ y |
| 2. | **recent** | p ___ ___ t |
| 3. | **ancient** | c o ___ ___ ___ ___ ___ ___ ___ ___ r y |
| 4. | **vice** | v i ___ ___ ___ u e |
| 5. | **voluntary** | o b ___ ___ ___ ___ ___ ___ r y |
| 6. | **compulsory** | o p ___ ___ ___ ___ a l |
| 7. | **consent** | d i ___ ___ ___ n t |
| 8. | **indifferent** | c a ___ ___ ___ g |
| 9. | **elated** | m i ___ ___ ___ ___ ___ l e |
| 10. | **cheerful** | d o ___ ___ ___ s t |
| 11. | **lament** | c e ___ ___ ___ ___ ___ ___ e |
| 12. | **myriad** | f ___ w |
| 13. | **stupid** | c l ___ ___ ___ r |
| 14. | **animosity** | g o ___ ___ ___ ___ l l |
| 15. | **ambiguous** | o b ___ ___ ___ u s |
| 16. | **negate** | c ___ ___ ___ ___ r m |
| 17. | **prompt** | s ___ ___ w |
| 18. | **hostile** | f ___ ___ ___ ___ ___ l y |
| 19. | **correct** | f ___ ___ ___ e |
| 20. | **vague** | p r ___ ___ ___ s e |

## 53. Odd One Out

**Instruction:** Find which word is the odd one out. Cross it out.

| 1. | argument | disagreement | dispute | contract |
| 2. | control | conflict | manage | supervise |
| 3. | interrogate | investigate | question | answer |
| 4. | teach | learn | find out | discover |
| 5. | write | right | inscribe | note |
| 6. | sight | see | sea | look |
| 7. | dessert | abandon | desert | forsake |
| 8. | allow | permit | let | leave |
| 9. | forget | suffer | pain | discomfort |
| 10. | entertain | amuse | amulet | please |
| 11. | quest | mission | task | question |
| 12. | interact | petrified | socialise | communicate |
| 13. | dishonest | disbeliever | sceptic | unbeliever |
| 14. | typical | usual | regular | abnormal |
| 15. | scarce | copious | luxuriant | rampant |
| 16. | infamous | honourable | commendable | meritorious |
| 17. | despicable | contemptible | ignominious | philanthropy |
| 18. | censure | reprimand | reproach | culpability |
| 19. | affiliation | coalition | confederation | commemoration |
| 20. | allure | entice | aside | attract |

## 54. Synonym

**Instruction:** Write the matching synonym from the Word Bank on the blank.

**Word Bank**

| answer | retort | clumsy | ask | assault |
| petrified | unconventional | unbeliever | abominable | loyal |
| defame | slander | bountiful | detest | plaudit |
| allegation | acquit | munificence | laudable | tear |

1. awkward
2. besmirch
3. terrified
4. assail
5. ovation
6. abundant
7. reply
8. accusation
9. abhor
10. faithful
11. loathsome
12. exonerate
13. atheist
14. commendable
15. rejoinder
16. largesse
17. laceration
18. inquire
19. defame
20. eccentric

## 55. Hide and Seek

**Instruction:** Write the matching synonyms from the Word Bank underneath the words in bold.

**Word Bank**

| conceal | look for | cover | mask | scout |
| shield | quest | shroud | hunt | camouflage |
| envelop | pursue | secret | desire | bury |
| disguise | search | browse | root out | forage |

| **Hide** | **Seek** |
|---|---|
| | |
| | |
| | |
| | |
| | |
| | |
| | |
| | |
| | |
| | |

# 56. Odd One Out

**Instruction:** Find which word is the odd one out. Cross it out.

| | | | | |
|---|---|---|---|---|
| 1. | humble | modest | arrogant | submissive |
| 2. | blasphemy | curse | swear | bless |
| 3. | trivial | serious | unimportant | minor |
| 4. | gather | disperse | scatter | spread |
| 5. | foreigner | stranger | immigrant | native |
| 6. | strong | feeble | fearless | brave |
| 7. | enlarge | elongate | expand | shrink |
| 8. | guilty | innocent | culpable | convicted |
| 9. | repair | destroy | demolish | dismantle |
| 10. | forgiving | vengeful | vindictive | angry |
| 11. | disgusting | abominable | loathsome | lurch |
| 12. | calumny | libel | slander | abundant |
| 13. | disarray | messiness | dispatcher | disorderliness |
| 14. | loiter | dawdle | stall | hasten |
| 15. | diminutive | miniature | monumental | miniscule |
| 16. | insignificant | eminent | esteemed | famous |
| 17. | crazy | indolent | languid | lazy |
| 18. | abundant | scarce | bountiful | plenty |
| 19. | negligent | careless | careful | irresponsible |
| 20. | evaluate | appraise | assess | associate |

# 57. Yes or No Game

**Instructions:** Write "Yes" in Column B if the words in Column A are antonyms. If they are NOT antonyms, write "No" then write an antonym for the first word. Several antonyms are possible.

| Column A | Column B |
|---|---|
| 1. disturbed – peaceful | |
| 2. belligerent – bellicose | |
| 3. fractious – calm | |
| 4. militant – militia | |
| 5. consensus – agreement | |
| 6. harmony – incompatibility | |
| 7. unanimity – difference | |
| 8. truce – peace | |
| 9. agree – concur | |
| 10. ameliorate – worsen | |
| 11. subdue – put down | |
| 12. relief – burden | |
| 13. appease – provoke | |
| 14. resolve – absolve | |
| 15. yearn – covet | |
| 16. adversity – difficulty | |
| 17. transparent – opaque | |
| 18. virtue – vice | |
| 19. defeat – victory | |
| 20. folly – wisdom | |

## 58. High and Low

**Instruction:** Write the matching synonyms from the Word Bank underneath the words in bold.

**Word Bank**

| towering | despicable | elevated | miserable | inferior |
|---|---|---|---|---|
| abject | tall | blue | soaring | upper |
| gloomy | down | above | base | lifted |
| escalated | heightened | lofty | downcast | sunken |

| **High** | **Low** |
|---|---|
| | |

## 59. Synonym

**Instruction:** Write the matching synonym from the Word Bank on the blank.

### Word Bank

| placate | palliate | addition | lure | wheedle |
| affable | disagreeable | vicious | incognito | affinity |
| appropriate | resist | antiquated | animosity | excuse |
| antipathy | repel | languid | imbue | outmoded |

1. passé _____
2. mollify _____
3. amicable _____
4. savage _____
5. alleviate _____
6. animus _____
7. apt _____
8. extension _____
9. antagonism _____
10. entice _____
11. rapport _____
12. extenuate _____
13. ancient _____
14. unpleasant _____
15. coax _____
16. anonymous _____
17. repulse _____
18. listless _____
19. permeate _____
20. oppose _____

# 60. Antonyms

**Instruction:** Complete the antonym of the word in bold.

|  |  |  |
|---|---|---|
| 1. | **respect** | d i _ _ _ _ _ _ c t |
| 2. | **restore** | b r _ _ k |
| 3. | **lengthen** | a b _ _ _ _ _ _ t e |
| 4. | **commence** | c o _ _ _ _ d e |
| 5. | **satisfy** | f r _ _ _ _ _ t e |
| 6. | **damage** | r e _ _ _ r |
| 7. | **restrained** | u n r _ _ _ _ _ _ n e d |
| 8. | **subtle** | c r _ _ e |
| 9. | **terminate** | b _ _ _ n |
| 10. | **fatigue** | e n _ _ _ y |
| 11. | **diminish** | i n _ _ _ _ s e |
| 12. | **overlook** | n o _ _ _ e |
| 13. | **reckless** | c a _ _ _ _ u s |
| 14. | **kind-hearted** | h e _ _ _ _ _ s s |
| 15. | **lose** | a c _ _ _ r e |
| 16. | **meek** | b _ _ d |
| 17. | **attentive** | i n _ _ _ _ _ _ _ v e |
| 18. | **thrive** | l a _ _ _ _ s h |
| 19. | **enhance** | d i _ _ _ _ s h |
| 20. | **calm** | t e _ _ _ _ _ _ _ a l |

# 61. Intense and Shallow

***Instruction:*** Write the matching synonyms from the Word Bank underneath the words in bold.

**Word Bank**

| profound | surface | superficial | ardent | foolish |
| unimportant | strong | rich | trivial | resonant |
| petty | frivolous | glib | serious | silly |
| extensive | flimsy | immeasurable | earnest | great |

| Intense | Shallow |
| --- | --- |
| | |

## 62. Yes or No Game

**Instructions:** Write "Yes" in Column B if the words in Column A are antonyms. If they are NOT antonyms, write "No" then write an antonym for the first word. Several antonyms are possible.

| Column A | Column B |
|---|---|
| 1. apathy – enthusiasm | |
| 2. lassitude – energetic | |
| 3. active – lethargic | |
| 4. flawless – blemished | |
| 5. shy – unabashed | |
| 6. heartlessness – indefinite | |
| 7. aroma – stink | |
| 8. profuse – sparse | |
| 9. gloomy – dark | |
| 10. hostile – violent | |
| 11. mischievous – malevolent | |
| 12. benevolent – unkind | |
| 13. aerate – deflate | |
| 14. decrease – decease | |
| 15. solemn – light hearted | |
| 16. egoistic – boastful | |
| 17. germane – appropriate | |
| 18. inimical – helpful | |
| 19. perfunctory – thorough | |
| 20. despondent – despair | |

# 63. Synonym

***Instruction:*** Write the matching synonym from the Word Bank on the blank.

**Word Bank**

| remorseful | apex | apropos | crude | authentic |
| apprentice | eloquent | tyrannical | capricious | determined |
| gruelling | squabble | augur | poise | parsimonious |
| hackneyed | amazing | banish | elated | elongate |

1. **summit** _____
2. **fickle** _____
3. **ecstatic** _____
4. **rudimentary** _____
5. **apt** _____
6. **arduous** _____
7. **contrite** _____
8. **bicker** _____
9. **prolong** _____
10. **articulate** _____
11. **bode** _____
12. **genuine** _____
13. **stingy** _____
14. **aplomb** _____
15. **novice** _____
16. **resolute** _____
17. **banal** _____
18. **autocratic** _____
19. **exile** _____
20. **remarkable** _____

# 64. Odd One Out

**Instruction:** Find which word is the odd one out. Cross it out.

| | | | | |
|---|---|---|---|---|
| 1. | amateur | professional | expert | knowledgeable |
| 2. | blunt | sharp | dull | rounded |
| 3. | calm | agitated | frustrated | angry |
| 4. | hopeless | despair | hope | desperate |
| 5. | doubt | attest | suspicion | hesitation |
| 6. | demand | ask | supply | request |
| 7. | agree | annoy | disturb | agitate |
| 8. | soothe | peaceful | calm | reproduce |
| 9. | fresh | recent | new | stale |
| 10. | grin | frown | smile | laugh |
| 11. | nasty | hasty | offensive | malicious |
| 12. | hazard | peril | disorder | danger |
| 13. | fail | succeed | achieve | accomplish |
| 14. | jump | leap | bounce | crawl |
| 15. | fraction | fraternity | fragment | snippet |
| 16. | favourite | dear | favoured | flavoured |
| 17. | blemished | flawless | intact | sound |
| 18. | prefer | choose | select | chomp |
| 19. | disagree | veto | prohibit | forbid |
| 20. | restriction | reduction | reproduction | cutback |

# 65. Synonyms

**Instruction:** Complete the synonym of the word in bold.

| 1. | **wrath** | a ___ ___ ___ r |
| 2. | **unnatural** | p r ___ ___ ___ ___ ___ ___ ___ u s |
| 3. | **calamity** | d i ___ ___ ___ ___ ___ r |
| 4. | **flinch** | w ___ ___ ___ e |
| 5. | **superficial** | s h ___ ___ ___ w |
| 6. | **stripe** | s t ___ ___ a k |
| 7. | **glitter** | s p ___ ___ ___ ___ l e |
| 8. | **rectify** | c o ___ ___ ___ c t |
| 9. | **affect** | i n ___ ___ ___ ___ ___ c e |
| 10. | **halt** | t e ___ ___ ___ ___ ___ t e |
| 11. | **perseverance** | t e ___ ___ ___ ___ t y |
| 12. | **baffle** | p e ___ ___ ___ ___ e x |
| 13. | **superfluous** | u n ___ ___ ___ ___ ___ ___ ___ r y |
| 14. | **treacherous** | d e ___ ___ ___ ___ ___ u l |
| 15. | **endeavour** | v e ___ ___ r e |
| 16. | **offensive** | i m ___ ___ ___ ___ n t |
| 17. | **supernatural** | o c ___ ___ ___ t |
| 18. | **monotonous** | t e ___ ___ ___ u s |
| 19. | **well-being** | w e ___ ___ ___ r e |
| 20. | **useless** | f ___ ___ ___ l e |

# 66. Dark and Light

**Instruction:** Write the matching synonyms from the Word Bank underneath the words in bold.

### Word Bank

| gloomy | illumination | black | pale | night |
|--------|--------------|-------|------|-------|
| brightness | obscure | shine | radiant | bright |
| grim | dismal | shady | glow | dreary |
| dim | nightfall | clear | fair | lamp |

| **Dark** | **Light** |
|----------|-----------|
|  |  |
|  |  |
|  |  |
|  |  |
|  |  |
|  |  |
|  |  |
|  |  |
|  |  |

## 67. Antonym

**Instruction:** Write the matching antonym from the Word Bank on the blank.

**Word Bank**

| purify | agreeable | restriction | delay | benevolence |
| accept | cruelty | assert | tractable | misunderstand |
| superior | indifferent | constructive | conquer | tardy |
| retain | love | eradicate | fake | strong |

1. **speed up** _____
2. **abolish** _____
3. **deny** _____
4. **obstinate** _____
5. **disagreeable** _____
6. **destructive** _____
7. **hate** _____
8. **reject** _____
9. **propagate** _____
10. **understand** _____
11. **surrender** _____
12. **authentic** _____
13. **mercy** _____
14. **malice** _____
15. **inferior** _____
16. **taint** _____
17. **interested** _____
18. **freedom** _____
19. **punctual** _____
20. **frail** _____

# 68. Odd One Out

**Instruction:** Find which word is the odd one out. Cross it out.

| #   | | | | |
|-----|---------------|---------------|---------------|--------------|
| 1.  | sleepy        | tired         | chewy         | drowsy       |
| 2.  | tiny          | little        | minor         | furry        |
| 3.  | rock          | music         | pebble        | stone        |
| 4.  | write         | right         | correct       | exact        |
| 5.  | same          | lame          | equal         | alike        |
| 6.  | noisy         | loud          | curious       | rowdy        |
| 7.  | auspicious    | inauspicious  | promising     | fortunate    |
| 8.  | aim           | goal          | target        | adjective    |
| 9.  | chant         | opportunity   | possibility   | chance       |
| 10. | sanguinity    | pessimism     | optimism      | hope         |
| 11. | reflect       | reverberate   | mirror        | centre       |
| 12. | recreate      | retire        | create        | reinvent     |
| 13. | resolution    | decision      | determination | hesitation   |
| 14. | figurative    | solve         | resolve       | figure       |
| 15. | guide         | bachelor      | usher         | escort       |
| 16. | determination | self-command  | insane        | willpower    |
| 17. | consume       | ingest        | intestine     | eat          |
| 18. | desire        | craving       | addiction     | adhesion     |
| 19. | consume       | devour        | down          | fully        |
| 20. | bloated       | starved       | ravenous      | famished     |

# 69. Yes or No Game

***Instructions:*** Write "Yes" in Column B if the words in Column A are antonyms. If they are NOT antonyms, write "No" then write an antonym for the first word. Several antonyms are possible.

| Column A | Column B |
|---|---|
| 1. fussy – proper | |
| 2. shallow – deep | |
| 3. untruthful – honest | |
| 4. bleak – cheerful | |
| 5. veneration – disrespect | |
| 6. bestow – beneath | |
| 7. remorse – regret | |
| 8. rustic – rural | |
| 9. pernicious – safe | |
| 10. frail – healthy | |
| 11. flair – inability | |
| 12. hazy – clear | |
| 13. precise – exact | |
| 14. serenity – anxiety | |
| 15. lustrous – dim | |
| 16. jocular – serious | |
| 17. melancholic – sadness | |
| 18. lavish – generous | |
| 19. mellifluous – melodious | |
| 20. bemoan – regret | |

## 70. Synonym

***Instruction:*** Write the matching synonym from the Word Bank on the blank.

**Word Bank**

| benevolent | deteriorate | confiscate | adulation | gloomy |
| toxic | limited | scorn | mischievous | immaculate |
| ameliorate | unpleasant | invulnerable | awe | great |
| paradox | grow | filthy | principal | decrease |

1. seize
2. admiration
3. poisonous
4. disrespect
5. charitable
6. naughty
7. improve
8. worsen
9. restricted
10. decline
11. sombre
12. colossal
13. develop
14. wonder
15. pristine
16. obnoxious
17. chief
18. contradiction
19. invincible
20. dirty

# 71. Open or Close

**Instruction:** Write the matching synonyms from the Word Bank underneath the words in bold.

**Word Bank**

| candid | clear | suspend | honest | finalise |
| finish | free | unlock | start | end |
| begin | initiate | commence | terminate | complete |
| conclude | direct | shut | stop | cease |

| **Open** | **Close** |
|---|---|
|  |  |
|  |  |
|  |  |
|  |  |
|  |  |
|  |  |
|  |  |
|  |  |
|  |  |
|  |  |

# 72. Odd One Out

**Instruction:** Find which word is the odd one out. Cross it out.

| | | | | |
|---|---|---|---|---|
| 1. | agony | anguish | comfort | pain |
| 2. | success | security | safety | sanctuary |
| 3. | myriad | scarcity | plenty | a lot |
| 4. | gratify | pleasure | satisfy | disappoint |
| 5. | puncture | hole | drill | punctual |
| 6. | fatigued | obsolete | tired | weary |
| 7. | ignite | excite | thrill | exhilarate |
| 8. | cultivate | labour | work | toil |
| 9. | accumulate | accentuate | gather | collect |
| 10. | deliver | expel | donate | receive |
| 11. | add | deduct | total | count |
| 12. | understand | comprehend | grasp | gradual |
| 13. | ameliorate | improve | antiquated | upgrade |
| 14. | instinctive | automatic | manual | reflexive |
| 15. | standard | normal | average | unique |
| 16. | consequential | diverse | significant | important |
| 17. | senseless | illogical | irrational | purposeful |
| 18. | present | tomorrow | later | afterward |
| 19. | unswerving | consistent | steady | irregular |
| 20. | justify | explain | refute | rationalize |

# 73. Yes or No Game

***Instructions:*** Write "Yes" in Column B if the words in Column A are antonyms. If they are NOT antonyms, write "No" then write an antonym for the first word. Several antonyms are possible.

| Column A | Column B |
|---|---|
| 1. defeat – triumph | |
| 2. folly – foolish | |
| 3. collect – acquire | |
| 4. imprudent – wise | |
| 5. peace – war | |
| 6. miser – spendthrift | |
| 7. magnify – diminish | |
| 8. vacate – occupy | |
| 9. discharge – deteriorate | |
| 10. acclaim – prestige | |
| 11. obscurity – villainy | |
| 12. famous – popular | |
| 13. intensify – amplify | |
| 14. allay – lessen | |
| 15. splurge – save | |
| 16. expend – store | |
| 17. porous – impervious | |
| 18. forgo – keep | |
| 19. wan – flushed | |
| 20. dense – compact | |

## 74. Vacant and Occupied

**Instruction:** Write the matching synonyms from the Word Bank underneath the words in bold.

### Word Bank

| empty | blank | engaged | void | free |
|---|---|---|---|---|
| deserted | preoccupied | vacuous | employed | uninhabited |
| taken | available | full | abandoned | devoid |
| working | inhabited | active | involved | busy |

| **Vacant** | **Occupied** |
|---|---|
| | |

## 75. Synonym

***Instruction:*** Write the matching synonym from the Word Bank on the blank.

**Word Bank**

| alluring | deception | demolition | garnish | faithfulness |
| secret | honoured | anguish | aversion | direct |
| lively | sympathy | conversant | friendly | skilful |
| destitute | instructive | unconventional | construct | gaiety |

1. **deceit** _____
2. **compassion** _____
3. **decorate** _____
4. **animated** _____
5. **talented** _____
6. **enticing** _____
7. **informed** _____
8. **distress** _____
9. **poor** _____
10. **destruction** _____
11. **forge** _____
12. **candid** _____
13. **confidential** _____
14. **eccentric** _____
15. **dislike** _____
16. **joy** _____
17. **fidelity** _____
18. **cordial** _____
19. **respected** _____
20. **didactic** _____

# 76. Odd One Out

**Instruction:** Find which word is the odd one out. Cross it out.

| | | | | |
|---|---|---|---|---|
| 1. | grief | anguish | guilt | sadness |
| 2. | imperious | superior | arrogant | triumph |
| 3. | inanimate | inert | lively | non-living |
| 4. | laughter | lament | cry | sorrow |
| 5. | hatred | melancholy | gloomy | depressed |
| 6. | pensive | thoughtful | contemplative | reckless |
| 7. | renown | honoured | misdeed | acclaimed |
| 8. | wild | domesticated | tame | docile |
| 9. | reprove | reprimand | scold | satisfy |
| 10. | impeach | disgrace | shame | ignominy |
| 11. | pleasant | fulsome | insincere | fawning |
| 12. | pillage | loot | plunder | valuable |
| 13. | rumour | vilify | rail | revile |
| 14. | haste | dawdle | drag | follow |
| 15. | atone | expiate | explain | make amends |
| 16. | reimburse | sell | repay | refund |
| 17. | boorish | ill-mannered | neanderthal | refined |
| 18. | forbid | formidable | impressive | terrific |
| 19. | restless | fidgety | jittery | relaxed |
| 20. | blunt | bland | flat | vapid |

# 77. New Year, Old Socks

**Instruction:** Write the matching synonyms from the Word Bank underneath the words in bold.

**Word Bank**

| original | current | former | contemporary | mature |
| novel | unprecedented | bygone | fresh | aged |
| worn | avant-garde | medieval | unknown | remote |
| modern | shabby | antique | archaic | past |

| **New Year** | **Old Socks** |
|---|---|
| | |

# 78. Yes or No Game

Instructions: Write "Yes" in Column B if the words in Column A are antonyms. If they are NOT antonyms, write "No" then write an antonym for the first word. Several antonyms are possible.

| | Column A | Column B |
|---|---|---|
| 1. | entire – partial | |
| 2. | brief – short | |
| 3. | broad – wide | |
| 4. | wicked – evil | |
| 5. | strange – creative | |
| 6. | harsh – pleasant | |
| 7. | restive – restless | |
| 8. | chide – praise | |
| 9. | deny – negate | |
| 10. | avert – prevent | |
| 11. | mutilate – mend | |
| 12. | luminous – gloomy | |
| 13. | interesting – riveting | |
| 14. | barren – fertile | |
| 15. | irritate – bother | |
| 16. | bewitch – repel | |
| 17. | inane – ingenious | |
| 18. | verify – invalidate | |
| 19. | approximate – estimate | |
| 20. | appreciate – recognize | |

# 79. Synonyms

**Instruction:** Complete the synonym of the word in bold.

| | | |
|---|---|---|
| 1. | **considerable** | s u _ _ _ _ _ _ _ a l |
| 2. | **demand** | r e _ _ _ _ t |
| 3. | **chuckle** | g i _ _ l e |
| 4. | **walk** | s t _ _ l l |
| 5. | **glance** | g l _ _ _ _ e |
| 6. | **love** | a f _ _ _ _ _ _ n |
| 7. | **mournful** | s o _ _ _ _ _ u l |
| 8. | **attractive** | p l _ _ _ _ n g |
| 9. | **purified** | r e _ _ _ e d |
| 10. | **marvellous** | e x _ _ _ _ _ _ _ _ r y |
| 11. | **tiny** | t e _ _ y |
| 12. | **compact** | p _ _ _ e d |
| 13. | **kind** | c o _ _ _ _ _ _ _ t e |
| 14. | **jocular** | f _ _ _ y |
| 15. | **amusing** | h u _ _ _ _ _ s |
| 16. | **funny** | w i _ _ y |
| 17. | **jovial** | j _ _ _ _ d |
| 18. | **stroll** | a m _ _ e |
| 19. | **astonishing** | s t u _ _ _ _ g |
| 20. | **respect** | a d _ _ _ _ _ _ o n |

## 80. Antonym

***Instruction:*** Write the matching antonym from the Word Bank on the blank.

**Word Bank**

| carelessness | simplicity | disturbed | antipathy | discouraged |
| dawdle | eloquence | sweet | comfort | respect |
| long | demotivate | poor | illegal | squander |
| happy | overlook | inadequate | fragrant | disorder |

1. **tranquil** _____
2. **scamper** _____
3. **distress** _____
4. **brief** _____
5. **hoard** _____
6. **conscientiousness** _____
7. **determined** _____
8. **rant** _____
9. **violate** _____
10. **rich** _____
11. **melancholy** _____
12. **observe** _____
13. **affection** _____
14. **malodorous** _____
15. **sour** _____
16. **complexity** _____
17. **sufficient** _____
18. **legal** _____
19. **structure** _____
20. **invigorate** _____

# 81. You May Be Right, But You Could Be Wrong

**Instruction:** Write the matching synonyms from the Word Bank underneath the words in bold.

## Word Bank

| misdeed | just | indictable | accurate | erroneous |
| equitable | upright | unlawful | virtuous | righteous |
| illicit | lawless | inaccurate | offence | fair |
| goodness | privilege | illegal | entitlement | faulty |

| **Right** | **Wrong** |
|---|---|
| | |
| | |
| | |
| | |
| | |
| | |
| | |
| | |
| | |
| | |

# 82. Odd One Out

**Instruction:** Find which word is the odd one out. Cross it out.

| | | | | |
|---|---|---|---|---|
| 1. | awful | dire | dreaded | please |
| 2. | panic | chaos | fear | distraction |
| 3. | gross | ugly | gorgeous | hideous |
| 4. | sorrow | sadness | regret | joy |
| 5. | plucky | vulnerable | mettlesome | dauntless |
| 6. | wane | ebb | dwindle | eliminate |
| 7. | give | abandon | leave | quit |
| 8. | despair | hope | melancholy | desperation |
| 9. | lethargy | inactivity | languor | energising |
| 10. | intertwined | brave | fearless | intrepid |
| 11. | scared | quiver | shake | tremble |
| 12. | grieve | grief | mourn | propriety |
| 13. | blunder | blooper | bungle | bundle |
| 14. | fatigue | excavate | weary | exhaustion |
| 15. | hazardous | attention | danger | risky |
| 16. | danger | peril | risk | courage |
| 17. | dire | wrath | rage | ire |
| 18. | defection | authorise | desertion | withdrawal |
| 19. | bold | broken | valiant | valorous |
| 20. | accomplish | achieve | attainment | attire |

## 83. Synonyms

**Instruction:** Complete the synonym of the word in bold.

| 1. | **precious** | v a ___ ___ ___ ___ l e |
| 2. | **hostility** | a n ___ ___ ___ ___ ___ t y |
| 3. | **inquisitive** | q ___ ___ ___ ___ ___ ___ ___ i n g |
| 4. | **candid** | s t ___ ___ ___ ___ ___ ___ ___ ___ ___ ___ ___ d |
| 5. | **sovereignty** | a u ___ ___ ___ ___ m y |
| 6. | **approval** | a u ___ ___ ___ ___ ___ ___ ___ ___ ___ o n |
| 7. | **soothe** | r e ___ ___ ___ v e |
| 8. | **advantage** | b e ___ ___ ___ ___ t |
| 9. | **defeat** | f a ___ ___ ___ r e |
| 10. | **eminent** | s u ___ ___ ___ ___ o r |
| 11. | **gratification** | s a ___ ___ ___ ___ ___ ___ ___ o n |
| 12. | **leverage** | a d ___ ___ ___ ___ ___ e |
| 13. | **preference** | f a ___ ___ ___ r |
| 14. | **gain** | p ___ ___ ___ i t |
| 15. | **help** | s u ___ ___ ___ ___ t |
| 16. | **authority** | j ___ ___ ___ ___ ___ ___ ___ ___ o n |
| 17. | **victory** | t r ___ ___ ___ ___ h |
| 18. | **delight** | p l ___ ___ ___ ___ e |
| 19. | **thrill** | e x ___ ___ ___ ___ ___ n t |
| 20. | **horrible** | h o ___ ___ ___ ___ u s |

## 84. Synonyms

**Instruction:** Choose the synonym of the word in bold.

| | | | | | |
|---|---|---|---|---|---|
| 1. | **unique** | simple | allowed | alike | special |
| 2. | **vicious** | gentle | helpful | danger | cruel |
| 3. | **precious** | necessary | usual | valuable | simple |
| 4. | **bulky** | skinny | large | tender | sick |
| 5. | **assist** | attend | apply | help | intend |
| 6. | **criticise** | berate | prove | laud | enjoy |
| 7. | **advocate** | predict | pronounce | support | determine |
| 8. | **authorise** | verify | neglect | protect | empower |
| 9. | **relegate** | prevaricate | promote | revitalize | downgrade |
| 10. | **conquer** | surrender | descend | triumph | divide |
| 11. | **enormous** | large | light | thin | small |
| 12. | **instigate** | halt | cause | action | actual |
| 13. | **amnesty** | pardon | obsolete | vice | doom |
| 14. | **anxiety** | relief | harmony | unity | agitation |
| 15. | **charity** | gift | theft | generosity | corruption |
| 16. | **frosty** | sweltering | humid | arid | chilly |
| 17. | **wondrous** | unsurprising | astounding | expected | bland |
| 18. | **tyranny** | despotism | republican | conservative | democracy |
| 19. | **flourish** | forest | thrive | threshold | flowers |
| 20. | **pompous** | arrogant | advocate | artificial | aristocrat |

## 85. Yes or No Game

**Instructions:** Write "Yes" in Column B if the words in Column A are antonyms. If they are NOT antonyms, write "No" then write an antonym for the first word. Several antonyms are possible.

| | Column A | Column B |
|---|---|---|
| 1. | excruciating – painful | |
| 2. | ostracize – expel | |
| 3. | prodigious – dread | |
| 4. | reluctant – eager | |
| 5. | erudite - brilliant | |
| 6. | outlandish - conventional | |
| 7. | apparent – obvious | |
| 8. | casual – planned | |
| 9. | precise – accurate | |
| 10. | sagacious – insightful | |
| 11. | reputable – notorious | |
| 12. | relevant – customary | |
| 13. | pessimism – optimism | |
| 14. | exciting – beautiful | |
| 15. | yummy – gross | |
| 16. | miniature – miniscule | |
| 17. | recent – ancient | |
| 18. | vice – virtue | |
| 19. | compulsory – obligatory | |
| 20. | steadfast – determined | |

## 86. Rude and Polite

***Instruction:*** Write the matching synonyms from the Word Bank underneath the words in bold.

### Word Bank

| gracious | gallant | unmannered | genteel | coarse |
| disrespectful | uncivil | courteous | mannerly | discourteous |
| civil | cultivated | impolite | impertinent | civilised |
| offensive | solicitous | Ill-mannered | boorish | well-behaved |

| **Rude** | **Polite** |
|---|---|
|   |   |
|   |   |
|   |   |
|   |   |
|   |   |
|   |   |
|   |   |
|   |   |
|   |   |
|   |   |

# 87. Odd One Out

**Instruction:** Find which word is the odd one out. Cross it out.

| | | | | |
|---|---|---|---|---|
| 1. | trust | belief | faith | suspect |
| 2. | alter | change | amend | prescribe |
| 3. | correctable | rechargeable | reversible | revocable |
| 4. | entire | done | finished | complete |
| 5. | docile | submissive | tamed | lame |
| 6. | spend | frugal | sparing | thrifty |
| 7. | anticipate | inflammation | await | expect |
| 8. | facilitate | alleviate | easy-going | ease |
| 9. | amend | assist | help | aid |
| 10. | vacillate | subordinate | hesitate | fluctuate |
| 11. | sloppy | lazy | slovenly | meticulous |
| 12. | error | fault | mistake | regret |
| 13. | hover | halt | arrest | hold |
| 14. | plunder | loot | ransack | backpack |
| 15. | exhort | inspire | urge | entourage |
| 16. | conservative | affiliate | associate | consort |
| 17. | modest | deceitful | humble | decent |
| 18. | unbearable | intolerable | unendurable | endured |
| 19. | abbreviated | mitigate | relieved | alleviated |
| 20. | face | avoid | seek | confront |

## 88. Antonym

**Instruction:** Complete the antonym of the word in bold.

|  |  |  |
|---|---|---|
| 1. | **adult** | i m _ _ _ _ r e |
| 2. | **alleviate** | a g _ _ _ _ _ t e |
| 3. | **attractive** | r e _ _ _ _ _ v e |
| 4. | **disarrange** | a r _ _ _ _ e |
| 5. | **aggressive** | p e _ _ _ _ u l |
| 6. | **harmful** | h e _ _ _ u l |
| 7. | **applaud** | c r _ _ _ _ _ s e |
| 8. | **concerned** | u n _ _ _ _ _ _ _ e d |
| 9. | **together** | a p _ _ t |
| 10. | **atrocious** | w o _ _ _ _ _ u l |
| 11. | **susceptible** | r e _ _ _ _ _ n t |
| 12. | **closed** | a _ _ r |
| 13. | **calm** | a _ g _ y |
| 14. | **war** | p _ _ _ e |
| 15. | **dead** | a n _ _ _ _ e d |
| 16. | **unlucky** | f o _ _ _ _ _ t e |
| 17. | **lackadaisical** | e x _ _ _ e d |
| 18. | **sobriety** | i n _ _ _ _ _ _ _ _ o n |
| 19. | **dauntless** | s c _ _ _ d |
| 20. | **invincible** | v u _ _ _ _ _ _ l e |

89. Synonym

**Instruction:** Write the matching synonym from the Word Bank on the blank.

**Word Bank**

| gain | banality | giving | comply | quit |
|---|---|---|---|---|
| gaunt | exceptional | dismaying | startled | villainous |
| hasten | tawdry | query | mawkish | abundant |
| secretive | inspect | veritable | test | wonderful |

1. obey _____
2. furtive _____
3. plentiful _____
4. scrawny _____
5. hurry _____
6. obtain _____
7. cliché _____
8. shocked _____
9. cease _____
10. inquiry _____
11. disturbing _____
12. shoddy _____
13. exam _____
14. generous _____
15. examine _____
16. nefarious _____
17. marvellous _____
18. sappy _____
19. outstanding _____
20. authentic _____

## 90. Dangerous and Safe

***Instruction:*** Write the matching synonyms from the Word Bank underneath the words in bold.

**Word Bank**

| wild | threatening | uninjured | menacing | vicious |
|---|---|---|---|---|
| savage | alright | risky | shielded | perilous |
| impregnable | harmless | precarious | defended | daredevil |
| prudent | reckless | cautious | unhurt | secure |

| **Dangerous** | **Safe** |
|---|---|
| | |
| | |
| | |
| | |
| | |
| | |
| | |
| | |
| | |
| | |

# 91. Synonym

*Instruction:* Complete the synonym of the word in bold.

| | | |
|---|---|---|
| 1. | **pensive** | t h __ __ __ __ __ __ u l |
| 2. | **penitent** | r e __ __ __ __ __ __ u l |
| 3. | **cordial** | f r __ __ __ __ l y |
| 4. | **coarse** | r o __ __ h |
| 5. | **accumulate** | g a __ __ __ r |
| 6. | **conquer** | d e __ __ __ t |
| 7. | **uncommon** | u n __ __ __ a l |
| 8. | **bliss** | h a __ __ __ __ __ s s |
| 9. | **mischievous** | p l __ __ __ __ l |
| 10. | **assess** | e s __ __ __ __ __ e |
| 11. | **brag** | b o __ __ t |
| 12. | **virtuous** | n __ __ __ e |
| 13. | **cover up** | c o __ __ __ __ l |
| 14. | **rue** | r e __ __ __ t |
| 15. | **peculiar** | s t __ __ __ __ e |
| 16. | **thrive** | f l __ __ __ __ s h |
| 17. | **disinfect** | s t __ __ __ __ __ s e |
| 18. | **virtuous** | r i __ __ __ __ __ u s |
| 19. | **resemble** | m i __ __ __ r |
| 20. | **refrain** | f o __ __ __ a r |

## 92. Yes or No Game

**Instructions:** Write "Yes" in Column B if the words in Column A are antonyms. If they are NOT antonyms, write "No" then write an antonym for the first word. Several antonyms are possible.

| | Column A | Column B |
|---|---|---|
| 1. | prompt – delayed | |
| 2. | candid – slow | |
| 3. | intrepid – wholesome | |
| 4. | hesitant – barren | |
| 5. | perspicuous – benevolent | |
| 6. | embrace – forefather | |
| 7. | meek – humble | |
| 8. | fragrant – stinky | |
| 9. | frail – fit | |
| 10. | obscene – fictitious | |
| 11. | decent – allude | |
| 12. | despondent – hopeful | |
| 13. | deserted – inhabited | |
| 14. | aversion – fondness | |
| 15. | impudence – desperation | |
| 16. | jubilant – melancholic | |
| 17. | defer – deft | |
| 18. | cease – begin | |
| 19. | cunning – prudent | |
| 20. | persistent – crass | |

# 93. You Can Laugh All You Want, or Cry Me a River

**Instruction:** Write the matching synonyms from the Word Bank underneath the words in bold.

### Word Bank

| chuckle | weep | sob | chortle | giggle |
| wail | joke | smirk | jest | shout |
| shriek | cackle | whine | guffaw | mourn |
| mock | howl | titter | lament | whimper |

**Laugh**                                              **Cry**

## 94. Synonym

**Instruction:** Write the matching synonym from the Word Bank on the blank.

**Word Bank**

| hermetic | evaporate | classy | apathetic | solicit |
| irresolute | setback | align | uneducated | disclose |
| inertia | prolific | abundance | abandon | buoyant |
| chief | affable | habitual | empathetic | join |

1. vaporise _____
2. ask for _____
3. reversal _____
4. illiterate _____
5. inactivity _____
6. fertile _____
7. desert _____
8. principal _____
9. friendly _____
10. link _____
11. airtight _____
12. indifferent _____
13. elegant _____
14. usual _____
15. reveal _____
16. upbeat _____
17. plethora _____
18. compassionate _____
19. indecisive _____
20. line up _____

## 95. Too Far or Very Near

**Instruction:** Write the matching synonyms from the Word Bank underneath the words in bold.

**Word Bank**

| imminent | nearby | distant | remote | close |
| isolated | forthcoming | faraway | almost | removed |
| away | adjacent | outlying | godforsaken | further |
| afar | accessible | proximate | approaching | immediate |

| **Far** | **Near** |
|---------|----------|
|         |          |
|         |          |
|         |          |
|         |          |
|         |          |
|         |          |
|         |          |
|         |          |
|         |          |
|         |          |

# 96. Synonym

**Instruction:** Complete the synonym of the word in bold.

| 1. | sterile | b a ___ ___ ___ n |
| 2. | tender | c ___ ___ ___ g |
| 3. | contemplate | c o ___ ___ ___ e r |
| 4. | resentment | b i t ___ ___ ___ ___ ___ s s |
| 5. | amend | r e ___ ___ ___ e |
| 6. | disclosure | r e v ___ ___ ___ ___ ___ o n |
| 7. | expel | b a ___ ___ ___ h |
| 8. | berate | c e ___ ___ ___ ___ e |
| 9. | imbecility | s ___ ___ ___ ___ ___ ___ t y |
| 10. | rustic | r ___ ___ ___ l |
| 11. | collusion | a g ___ ___ ___ ___ ___ n t |
| 12. | invalidate | n e ___ ___ ___ e |
| 13. | peril | d ___ ___ ___ ___ r |
| 14. | vindictive | v ___ ___ ___ ___ ___ u l |
| 15. | hostility | e n ___ ___ t y |
| 16. | reject | d i s ___ ___ ___ ___ v e |
| 17. | remorse | r ___ ___ ___ e t |
| 18. | weary | f a ___ ___ ___ ___ e d |
| 19. | shake | t r ___ ___ ___ e |
| 20. | salient | i m ___ ___ ___ ___ ___ n t |

# 97. Short and Tall

**Instruction:** Write the matching synonyms from the Word Bank underneath the words in bold.

**Word Bank**

| tiny | squat | brief | towering | colossal |
| elevated | fleeting | teeny | altitudinous | wee |
| petite | diminutive | monstrous | compact | giant |
| steep | lofty | gigantic | high | miniscule |

**Short**                                        **Tall**

## 98. Yes or No Game

**Instructions:** Write "Yes" in Column B if the words in Column A are antonyms. If they are NOT antonyms, write "No" then write an antonym for the first word. Several antonyms are possible.

| | Column A | Column B |
|---|---|---|
| 1. | amicable – hearten | |
| 2. | ample – enough | |
| 3. | meagre – sufficient | |
| 4. | baleful – beneficent | |
| 5. | deference – courteous | |
| 6. | dormant – active | |
| 7. | dubious – confident | |
| 8. | unprecedented – common | |
| 9. | deception – falsehood | |
| 10. | innumerable – countable | |
| 11. | immeasurable – delayed | |
| 12. | perpetual – constant | |
| 13. | evoke – elicit | |
| 14. | flimsy – powerful | |
| 15. | garish – gaudy | |
| 16. | indict – advocate | |
| 17. | untried – ancient | |
| 18. | veracity – misinformation | |
| 19. | latent – obvious | |
| 20. | reparation - restitution | |

## 99. Synonym

*Instruction:* Write the matching synonym from the Word Bank on the blank.

**Word Bank**

| fragile | apprise | consensus | treason | loyal |
| amiable | lucent | ravaged | ephemeral | filthy |
| anonymous | extravagant | hinder | relish | vague |
| sage | delirious | squander | abrogate | submissive |

1. short-lived _____
2. impede _____
3. destroyed _____
4. inform _____
5. dirty _____
6. spendthrift _____
7. devoted _____
8. enjoy _____
9. unknown _____
10. agreement _____
11. delicate _____
12. luminous _____
13. unclear _____
14. waste _____
15. friendly _____
16. repeal _____
17. betrayal _____
18. hallucinating _____
19. servile _____
20. wise _____

# 100. Remember Me or Forget All About Me

**Instruction:** Write the matching synonyms from the Word Bank underneath the words in bold.

### Word Bank

| recall | recollect | place | learn | ignore |
| commemorate | neglect | remind | overlook | memorise |
| unlearn | erase | reminisce | blank | elude |
| retrieve | neglect | recapture | escape | misremember |

| **Remember** | **Forget** |
|---|---|
| | |
| | |
| | |
| | |
| | |
| | |
| | |
| | |
| | |
| | |

# Answer Key

1. 1.mend 2.foe 3.dislike 4.frown 5.fresh 6.dangerous 7.finish 8.future 9.laugh 10.easy 11.worse 12.unknown 13.dead 14.leave 15.unstable 16.end 17.doubt 18.colourful 19.tiny 20.same

2. Happy (cheery, gleeful, merry, sunny, upbeat, grinning, beaming, jolly, buoyant, contented)
   Sad (sorrowful, miserable, depressed, blue, down, gloomy, glum, woeful, forlorn, woebegone)

3. 1.away 2.copious 3.greatest 4.warped 5.receive 6.disclose 7.transparent 8.tranquil 9.friendly 10.careful 11.omit 12.correct 13.very important 14.delicious 15.puzzling 16.solidarity 17.repay 18.area 19.bypass 20.frank

4. 1.yes 2.no 3.yes 4.yes 5.no 6.yes 7.no 8.no 9.no 10.yes 11.yes 12.no 13.yes 14.no 15.no 16.yes 17.yes 18.yes 19.yes 20.no

5. Strong (athletic, powerful, forceful, tough, solid, fit, firm, brawny, redoubtable, stout)
   Weak (fragile, sick, delicate, fatigued, infirm, spent, debilitated, feeble, rickety, flimsy)

6. 1.occur 2.deny 3.rough 4.worth 5.ancient 6.silent 7.carpet 8.enquire 9.author 10.blend 11.liberty 12.monotony 13.insert 14.sugary 15.tiny 16.unwell 17.deceive 18.courageous 19.honesty 20.continue

7. Lots (plenty, many, tons, heaps, myriad, copious, dozens, several, piles, abundant)
   Few (meagre, lean, infrequent, sparse, rare, scarce, slight, scant, paltry, little)

8. 1.guilty 2.bold 3.complicated 4.extravagance 5.sharp 6.sterile 7.quiet 8.hazardous 9.discourteous 10.accurate 11.energetic 12.treacherous 13.question 14.aimlessness 15.pull 16.enemy 17.never 18.occupied 19.obscure 20.rare

9.  1.reject 2.adjust 3.achieve 4.adolescent 5.stray 6.bare 7.draught 8.shrink 9.awful 10.sob 11.divine 12.above 13.smooth 14.once 15.scream 16.scrawny 17.rigid 18.sickly 19.filled 20.seldom

10. Beautiful (comely, alluring, exquisite, attractive, pleasant, dazzling, enthralling, stunning, gorgeous, lovely)
    Ugly (hideous, unsightly, ghastly, nasty, repellent, repulsive, deformed, awful, grotesque, disgusting)

11. 1.absolve 2.contrast 3.fluctuate 4.generate 5.mediate 6.traumatic 7.beneficial 8.valid 9.mandatory 10.dilemma 11.perception 12.scrutiny 13.elude 14.infamous 15.alternative 16.mistake 17.evaluate 18.derive 19.mortify 20.sabotage

12. 1.trust 2.voracious 3.pleasure 4.diligent 5.reject 6.significant 7.empty 8.pleasant 9.boast 10.grant 11.fast 12.sleepy 13.drowsy 14.tidy 15.mushy 16.upset 17.masculine 18.malicious 19.teenager 20.mature

13. Forbid (restrain, ban, preclude, veto, block, sanction, disallow, prohibit, interdict, outlaw, proscribe)
    Permit (enjoin, authorise, permit, approve, entitle, grant, let, empower, allow)

14. 1.deduct 2.flourish 3.deficient 4.immune 5.enthusiastic 6.converge 7.leave 8.begin 9.tranquillity 10.carnivore 11.implicit 12.diurnal 13.inaccurate 14.formidable 15.inclusive 16.protagnonist 17.climb 18.agitation 19.virtuoso 20.outgoing

15. 1.modest 2.resilient 3.graceful 4.repel 5.bearded 6.leave 7.outgoing 8.accept 9.plain 10.luxury 11.give 12.present 13.offense 14.deteriorate 15.abandon 16.narrow 17.safe 18.vanish 19.prevent 20.useless

16. 1.modest 2.deafening 3.contemporary 4.wealthy 5.cynic 6.untruth 7.bucket 8.wait 9.unhappy 10.protect 11.quick-witted 12.strong 13.vigilant 14.revelation 15.brawl 16.organise 17.divert 18.command 19.grasp 20.accept

17. Smart (clever, savvy, perceptive, brainy, alert, sharp, bright, intelligent, genius, brilliant)
    Stupid (ignorant, foolish, ludicrous, thick, dumb, mindless, brainless, imbecile, silly, dummy)

18. 1.yes 2.no 3.no 4.no 5.no 6.no 7.no 8.yes 9.no 10.yes 11.yes 12.no 13.yes 14.yes 15.no 16.no 17.yes 18.yes 19.no 20.no

19. 1.hate 2.bellitle 3.forgive 4.brother 5.allow 6.immorality 7.push 8.desire 9.present 10.classroom 11.error 12.prediction 13.liability 14.letter 15.ancient 16.enthusiastic 17.scepticism 18.promptness 19.attic 20.remorse

20. Big (substantial, huge, great, enormous, mighty, gigantic, colossal, stupendous, massive, jumbo)
    Small (diminutive, petite, tiny, slight, compact, insignificant, miniature, minuscule, microscopic, baby)

21. 1.irrelevant 2.empty 3.satisfied 4.temporary 5.sparse 6.original 7.trivial 8.true 9.demand 10.white 11.increase 12.vacant 13.merciful 14.stay 15.against 16.con 17.concrete 18.specific 19.night 20.melt

22. 1.include 2.purchase 3.fright 4.seat 5.delayed 6.inner 7.confess 8.additional 9.carry 10.seize 11.terror 12.come 13.actual 14.movement 15.ignore 16.adore 17.flunk 18.prepared 19.greatest 20.alike

23. Clean (unsoiled, washed, tidy, pure, spotless, scrubbed, unstained, sanitary, hygienic, cleansed)
    Dirty (filthy, grimy, mucky, nasty, greasy, contaminated, icky, stained, foul, obscene)

24. 1.uphill 2.take-off 3.theory 4.asset 5.deport 6.allegiance 7.exit 8.land 9.different 10.absence 11.import 12.liquid 13.safety 14.primary 15.belief 16.inferior 17.anonymous 18.departure 19.proof 20.proximity

25. 1.split 2.plain 3.triumph 4.holiday 5.belongings 6.distress 7.cease 8.brutality 9.elderly 10.ballot 11.obtain 12.country 13.learn 14.current 15.quest 16.youthful 17.malevolent 18.inform 19.movie 20.incorrect

26. Similar (comparable, equivalent, matching, akin, alike, related, homogeneous, resembling, close, analogous)
Different (discrete, disparate, individual, dissimilar, incompatible, unusual, contrasting, distinct, inconsistent, diverse)

27. 1.correct 2.humid 3.there 4.solid 5.maximum 6.nobody 7.yesterday 8.absent 9.centre 10.approximately 11.alive 12.outrageous 13.divide 14.heaven 15.bottom 16.servant 17.public 18.native 19.worst 20.learn

28. 1.sickness 2.dullness 3.jeopardy 4.sometimes 5.stink 6.boring 7.endangered 8.suffering 9.cautious 10.eager 11.forest 12.vindictive 13.scene 14.direct 15.loyalty 16.joy 17.insomnia 18.demonstrate 19.eradicate 20.forcefully

29. Fresh (new, natural, unspoiled, pristine, original, pure, unprocessed, clean, unpreserved, uncured)
Stale (old, rotten, spoiled, off, hardened, rancid, decayed, dry, musty, timeworn)

30. 1.outside 2.clean 3.book 4.wound 5.heal 6.musty 7.derive 8.apart 9.neighbour 10.finish 11.treacherous 12.monochrome 13.unicorn 14.superb 15.sunrise 16.inaugurate 17.prudent 18.proud 19.outburst 20.wreck

31. 1.yes 2.no 3.yes 4.no 5.no 6.yes 7.yes 8.yes 9.no 10.yes 11.no 12.no 13.no 14.no 15.no 16.no 17.yes 18.yes 19.yes 20.yes

32. Try (test, attempt, seek, strive, aspire, effort, taste, check, experiment, endeavour)
Quit (retire, withdraw, leave, abandon, cease, drop, resign, left, desert, discontinue)

33. 1.nice 2.complicated 3.pleased 4.loud 5.petite 6.woman 7.unhappy 8.enormous

9.fascinating 10.unusual 11.baggy 12.scorching 13.waste 14.absurd 15.huge 16.careful 17.disagree 18.brave 19.succeed 20.annoy

34. 1.die 2.partial 3.winter 4.clean 5.last 6.laugh 7.build 8.healthy 9.common 10.untrustworthy 11.destroy 12.soft 13.normal 14.fairness 15.peace 16.skinny 17.woman 18.youthful 19.close 20.country

35. Problem (trouble, issue, challenge, difficulty, complication, worry, nuisance, obstacle, concern, predicament)
Solution (result, answer, determination, finding, solving, key, explication, conclusion, resolution, explanation)

36. 1.nasty 2.thankful 3.accurate 4.sell 5.break 6.among 7.steel 8.dice 9.recede 10.friendly 11.fiction 12.commence 13.missile 14.shift 15.deluxe 16.condition 17.style 18.mushroom 19.heat 20.shiver

37. 1.distant 2.relative 3.pleasant 4.imposter 5.pull 6.cautious 7.spoils 8.suggest 9.extend 10.humble 11.brave 12.helpful 13.settle 14.deceive 15.dwell 16.meeting 17.tailored 18.distant 19.careless 20.blaze

38. Luck (fortune, chance, fate, destiny, serendipity, fortuity, providence, windfall, happenstance, fluke)
Misfortune (calamity, mishap, misery, catastrophe, tribulation, disaster, difficulty, hardship, tragedy, setback)

39. 1.neglect 2.sink 3.delight 4.master 5.common 6.calm 7.cowardice 8.compassionate 9.stupid 10.peace 11.guilty 12.obvious 13.boastful 14.interesting 15.expand 16.sweet 17.darkness 18.punish 19.initial 20.reject

40. 1.weak 2.hide 3.gather 4.adversity 5.brute 6.attentive 7.dissipate 8.kind 9.agitate 10.follow 11.result 12.fake 13.shortage 14.talk 15.emit 16.impure 17.brief 18.mercy 19.display 20.fair

41. Loud (noisy, deafening, boisterous, roaring, rowdy, blaring, clamorous, ear-splitting, thunderous, resounding)
Quiet (peace, tranquil, placid, subdued, pacify, still, hush, serene, soundless, silent)

42. 1.no 2.yes 3.yes 4.yes 5.no 6.yes 7.yes 8.no 9.yes 10.no 11.yes 12.no 13.no 14.yes 15.yes 16.yes 17.yes 18.yes 19.no 20.yes

43. 1.conflict 2.guest 3.upper 4.friendship 5.darling 6.disregard 7.smooth 8.misuse 9.receive 10.ribbon 11.plea 12.announce 13.unity 14.great 15.awake 16.traffic 17.povery 18.defeat 19.gross 20.gradual

44. 1.wealth 2.force 3.melody 4.watch 5.help 6.jump 7.prize 8.dazzling 9.careful 10.party 11.touch 12.finish 13.cash 14.shiny 15.gloomy 16.cramped 17.crunchy 18.wonder 19.bathe 20.success

45. Guilty (ashamed, responsible, culpable, sinful, blameable, convicted, criminal, repentant, remorseful, contrite)
Innocent (untainted, pure, naive, blameless, chaste, faultless, inoffensive, vindicated, acquitted, exonerated)

46. 1.mother 2.intellect 3.hit 4.brother 5.older 6.few 7.answer 8.short 9.wife 10.hopeful 11.chaos 12.asleep 13.cold 14.give up 15.changeable 16.earier 17.devil 18.adults 19.negative 20.none

47. 1.emergency 2.known 3.view 4.genuine 5.kind 6.stimulating 7.sweet 8.train 9.manage 10.terrible 11.cook 12.exaggerate 13.marvel 14.destroy 15.hit 16.wet 17.return 18.belittle 19.evening 20.nothing

48. 1.host 2.detailed 3.finite 4.reflection 5.incomparable 6.wicked 7.compound 8.fright 9.squeak 10.diminutive 11.neutral 12.default 13.rigid 14.stretch 15.determined 16.mundane 17.advertise 18.fragile 19.irrelevant 20.impediment

49. 1.soft 2.find 3.above 4.warm 5.tall 6.organised 7.light 8.early 9.full 10.far 11.dry 12.enormous 13.far 14.light 15.narrow 16.near 17.slow 18.full 19.dumb 20.entrance

50. Friend (buddy, companion, ally, comrade, mate, pal, associate, fellow, partner, supporter)
    Foe (enemy, opponent, rival, attacker, competitor, antagonist, adversary, challenger, arch-enemy, disputant)

51. 1.no 2.yes 3.no 4.yes 5.yes 6.yes 7.no 8.yes 9.yes 10.no 11.no 12.no 13.no 14.no 15.yes 16.yes 17.yes 18.yes 19.yes 20.yes

52. 1.deny 2.past 3.contemporary 4.virtue 5.obligatory 6.optional 7.dissent 8.caring 9.miserable 10.downcast 11.celebrate 12.few 13.clever 14.goodwill 15.obvious 16.confirm 17.slow 18.friendly 19.false 20.precise

53. 1.contract 2.conflict 3.answer 4.teach 5.right 6.sea 7.dessert 8.leave 9.forget 10.amulet 11.question 12.petrified 13.dishonest 14.abnormal 15.scarce 16.infamous 17.philanthropy 18.culpability 19.commemoration 20.aside

54. 1.clumsy 2.defame 3.petrified 4.assault 5.plaudit 6.bountiful 7.answer 8.allegation 9.detest 10.loyal 11.abominable 12.acquit 13.unbeliever 14.laudable 15.retort 16.munificence 17.tear 18.ask 19.slander 20.unconventional

55. Hide (conceal, cover, mask, shield, shroud, camouflage, envelop, secret, disguise, bury)
    Seek (look for, scout, browse, hunt, pursue, desire, quest, search, root out, forage)

56. 1.arrogant 2.bless 3.serious 4.gather 5.native 6.feeble 7.shrink 8.innocent 9.repair 10.forgiving 11.lurch 12.abundant 13.dispatcher 14.hasten 15.monumental 16.insignificant 17.crazy 18.scarce 19.careful 20.associate

57. 1.yes 2.no 3.yes 4.no 5.no 6.yes 7.yes 8.no 9.no 10.yes 11.no 12.yes 13.yes 14.no 15.no 16.no 17.yes 18.yes 19.yes 20.yes

58. High (towering, elevated, tall, soaring, upper, lifted, above, escalated, heightened, lofty)
Low (despicable, miserable, inferior, abject, blue, gloomy, down, downcast, base, sunken)

59. 1.outmoded 2.placate 3.affable 4.vicious 5.palliate 6.animosity 7.appropriate 8.addition 9.antipathy 10.lure 11.affinity 12.excuse 13.antiquated 14.disagreeable 15.wheedle 16. incognito 17.repel 18.languid 19.imbue 20.resist

60. 1.disrespect 2.break 3.abbreviate 4.conclude 5.frustrate 6.repair 7.unrestraint 8.crude 9.begin 10.energy 11.increase 12.notice 13.cautious 14.heartless 15.acquire 16.bold 17.inattentive 18.languish 19.diminish 20.temperamental

61. Intense (ardent, profound, strong, rich, resonant, serious, extensive, immeasurable, earnest, great)
Shallow (surface, superficial, foolish, unimportant, trivial, petty, glib, silly, flimsy, frivolous)

62. 1.yes 2.yes 3.yes 4.yes 5.yes 6.no 7.yes 8.yes 9.no 10.no 11.no 12.yes 13.yes 14.no 15.yes 16.no 17.no 18.yes 19.yes 20.no

63. 1.apex 2.capricious 3.elated 4.crude 5.apropos 6.grueling 7.remorseful 8.squabble 9.elongate 10.eloquent 11.augur 12.authentic 13.parsimonious 14.poise 15.apprentice 16.determined 17.hackneyed 18.tyrannical 19.banish 20.amazing

64. 1.amateur 2.sharp 3.calm 4.hope 5.attest 6.supply 7.agree 8.reproduce 9.stale 10.frown 11.hasty 12.disorder 13.fail 14.crawl 15.fraternity 16.flavoured 17.blemished 18.chomp 19.disagree 20.reproduction

65.  1.anger 2.pretentious 3.disaster 4.wince 5.shallow 6.streak 7.sparkle 8.correct 9.influence 10.terminate 11.tenacity 12.perplex 13.unnecessary 14.deceitful 15.venture 16.impudent 17.occult 18.tedious 19.welfare 20.futile

66.  Dark (gloomy, black, night, obscure, grim, dismal, shady, dreary, dim, nightfall)
Light (illumination, pale, brightness, shine, radiant, bright, glow, clear, fair, lamp)

67.  1.delay 2.retain 3.assert 4.tractable 5.agreeable 6.constructive 7.love 8.accept 9.eradicate 10.misunderstand 11.conquer 12.fake 13.cruelty 14.benevolence 15.superior 16.purify 17.indifferent 18.restriction 19.tardy 20.strong

68.  1.chewy 2.furry 3.music 4.write 5.lame 6.curious 7.inauspicious 8.adjective 9.chant 10.pessimism 11.centre 12.retire 13.hesitation 14.figurative 15.bachelor 16.insane 17.intestine 18.adhesion 19.fully 20.bloated

69.  1.no 2.yes 3.yes 4.yes 5.yes 6.no 7.no 8.no 9.yes 10.yes 11.yes 12.yes 13.no 14.yes 15.yes 16.yes 17.no 18.no 19.no 20.no

70.  1.confiscate 2.adulation 3.toxic 4.scorn 5.benevolent 6.mischievous 7.ameliorate 8.deteriorate 9.limited 10.decrease 11.gloomy 12.great 13.grow 14.awe 15.immaculate 16.unpleasant 17.principal 18.paradox 19.invulnerable 20.filthy

71.  Open (candid, clear, honest, free, unlock, start, begin, initiate, commence, direct)
Close (suspend, finalise, finish, end, terminate, complete, conclude, shut, stop, cease)

72.  1.comfort 2.success 3.scarcity 4.disappoint 5.punctual 6.obsolete 7.ignite 8.cultivate 9.accentuate 10.receive 11.deduct 12.gradual 13.antiquated 14.manual 15.unique 16.diverse 17.purposeful 18.present 19.irregular 20.refute

73.  1.yes 2.no 3.no 4.yes 5.yes 6.yes 7.yes 8.yes 9.no 10.no 11.no 12.no 13.no 14.no 15.yes 16.yes 17.yes 18.yes 19.yes 20.no

74. Vacant (empty, blank, void, free, deserted, vacuous, uninhabited, available, abandoned, devoid)
    Occupied (busy, engaged, preoccupied, employed, taken, full, working, inhabited, active, involved)

75. 1.deception 2.sympathy 3.garnish 4.lively 5.skillful 6.alluring 7.conversant 8.anguish 9.destitute 10.demolition 11.construct 12.direct 13.secret 14.unconventional 15.aversion 16.gaiety 17.faithful 18.friendly 19.honoured 20.instructive

76. 1.guilt 2.triumph 3.lively 4.laughter 5.hatred 6.reckless 7.misdeed 8.wild 9.satisfy 10.impeach 11.pleasant 12.valuable 13.rumour 14.haste 15.explain 16.sell 17.refined 18.forbid 19.relaxed 20.blunt

77. New (original, current, contemporary, novel, unprecedented, fresh, avant-garde, unknown, modern)
    Old (former, remote, shabby, mature, bygone, aged, worn, medieval, antique, archaic, past)

78. 1.yes 2.no 3.no 4.no 5.no 6.yes 7.yes 8.yes 9.no 10.no 11.yes 12.yes 13.no 14.yes 15.no 16.yes 17.yes 18.yes 19.no 20.no

79. 1.substantial 2.request 3.giggle 4.stroll 5.glimpse 6.affection 7.sorrowful 8.pleasing 9.refined 10.extraordinary 11.teeny 12.packed 13.considerate 14.funny 15.humorous 16.witty 17.jocund 18.amble 19.stunning 20.admiration

80. 1.disturbed 2.dawdle 3.comfort 4.long 5.squander 6. carelessness 7.discouraged 8.eloquence 9.respect 10.poor 11.happy 12.overlook 13.antipathy 14.fragrant 15.sweet 16.simplicity 17.inadequate 18.illegal 19.disorder 20.demotivate

81. Right (just, accurate, equitable, upright, virtuous, righteous, fair, goodness, privilege, entitlement)
    Wrong (misdeed, indictable, erroneous, unlawful, illicit, lawless, inaccurate, offence, illegal, faulty)

82. 1.please 2.distraction 3.gorgeous 4.joy 5.vulnerable 6.eliminate 7.give 8.hope 9.energising 10.intertwined 11.scared 12.propriety 13.bundle 14.excavate 15.attention 16.courage 17.dire 18.authorise 19.broken 20.attire

83. 1.valuable 2.animosity 3.questioning 4.straightforward 5.autonomy 6.authorisation 7.relieve 8.benefit 9.failure 10.superior 11.satisfaction 12.advantage 13.favour 14.profit 15.support 16.jursidiction 17.triumph 18.pleasure 19.excitement 20.horrendous

84. 1.special 2.cruel 3.valuable 4.large 5.help 6.berate 7.support 8.empower 9.downgrade 10.triumph 11.large 12.cause 13.pardon 14.agitation 15.generosity 16.chilly 17.astounding 18.despotism 19.thrive 20.arrogant

85. 1.no 2.no 3.no 4.yes 5.no 6.yes 7.no 8.yes 9.no 10.no 11.yes 12.no 13.yes 14.no 15.yes 16.no 17.yes 18.yes 19.no 20.no

86. Rude (unmannered, coarse, disrespectful, uncivil, discourteous, impolite, impertinent, offensive, ill-mannered, boorish)
Polite (gracious, gallant, genteel, civil, courteous, cultivated, civilised, mannerly, solicitous, well-behaved)

87. 1.suspect 2.prescribe 3.rechargeable 4.entire 5.lame 6.spend 7.inflammation 8.easy-going 9.amend 10.subordinate 11.meticulous 12.regret 13.hover 14.backpack 15.entourage 16.conservative 17.deceitful 18.endured 19.abbreviated 20.avoid

88. 1.immature 2.aggravate 3.repulsive 4.arrange 5.peaceful 6.helpful 7.criticise 8.unconcerned 9.apart 10.wonderful 11.resistant 12.ajar 13.angry 14.peace 15.animated 16.fortunate 17.excited 18.intoxication 19.scared 20.vulnerable

89. 1.comply 2.secretive 3.abundant 4.gaunt 5.hasten 6.gain 7.banality 8.startled 9.quit 10.query 11.dismaying 12.tawdry 13.test 14.giving 15.inspect 16.villainous 17.wonderful 18.mawkish 19.exceptional 20.veritable

90. Dangerous (wild, threatening, menacing, vicious, savage, risky, perilous, daredevil, reckless, precarious)
    Safe (uninjured, alright, shielded, impregnable, harmless, defended, prudent, cautious, unhurt, secure)

91. 1.thoughtful 2.remorseful 3.friendly 4.rough 5.gather 6.defeat 7.unusual 8.happiness 9.playful 10.estimate 11.boast 12.noble 13.conceal 14.regret 15.strange 16.flourish 17.sterilise 18.righteous 19.mirror 20.forbear

92. 1.yes 2.no 3.no 4.no 5.no 6.no 7.no 8.yes 9.yes 10.no 11.no 12.yes 13.yes 14.yes 15.no 16.yes 17.no 18.yes 19.no 20.no

93. Laugh (chuckle, chortle, giggle, joke, smirk, jest, cackle, guffaw, mock, titter)
    Cry (weep, sob, wail, shout, shriek, whine, mourn, lament, whimper, howl)

94. 1.evaporate 2.solicit 3.setback 4.uneducated 5.inertia 6.prolific 7.abandon 8.chief 9.affable 10.join 11.hermetic 12.apathetic 13.classy 14.habitual 15.disclose 16.buyoant 17.abundance 18.empathetic 19.irresolute 20.align

95. Far (distant, remote, isolated, faraway, removed, away, outlying, godforsaken, afar, further)
    Near (imminent, nearby, close, almost, forthcoming, adjacent, accessible, proximate, approaching, immediate)

96. 1.barren 2.caring 3.consider 4.bitterness 5.revise 6.revelation 7.banish 8.censure 9.stupidity 10.rural 11.agreement 12.negate 13.danger 14.vengeful 15.enmity 16.disapprove 17.regret 18.fatigued 19.tremble 20.important

97. Short (tiny, squat, miniscule, brief, fleeting, teeny, wee, petite, diminutive, compact)
    Tall (towering, colossal, elevated, altitudinous, monstrous, giant, steep, lofty, gigantic, high)

98. 1.no 2.no 3.yes 4.yes 5.no 6.yes 7.yes 8.yes 9.no 10.yes 11.no 12.no 13.no 14.yes 15.no 16.yes 17.no 18.yes 19.yes 20.no

99. 1.ephemeral 2.hinder 3.ravaged 4.apprise 5.filthy 6.extravagant 7.loyal 8.relish 9.anonymous 10.consensus 11.fragile 12.lucent 13.vague 14.squander 15.amiable 16.abrogate 17.treason 18.delirious 19.submissive 20.sage

100. Remember (recall, recollect, place, learn, commemorate, remind, memorise, reminisce, retrieve, recapture)
Forget (ignore, neglect, overlook, unlearn, erase, blank, elude, neglect, escape, misremember)

Printed in Great Britain
by Amazon